C000023916

CENTURIONS

ANDRE
DEUTSCH

CENTURIONS

A PHOTOGRAPHIC TRIBUTE TO 100 MEN & WOMEN WHO HAVE CHANGED THE FACE OF 20TH-CENTURY BRITAIN

BY
CAROLYN DJANOGLY

WITH A FOREWORD
BY
ASA BRIGGS

In association with

SG

ASSET MANAGEMENT

For my parents, Lee and Maurice,
who taught me the meaning of family

PORTRAITS BY CAROLYN DJANOGLY

Text by Carolyn Djanogly and Natalie Walsh
assisted by Jane Merkin

With grateful thanks to KJP for their
assistance in supplying the Rolleiflex 6008
Integral camera, Bowens studio flash
equipment and Ilford HP5 film.

First published in 1999 by
André Deutsch Limited
76 Dean Street
London W1V 5HA
www.vci.co.uk

A catalogue record for this book is available from the British
Library.

ISBN 0 233 99753 9

Design by SMITH
Printed by E. G. Bond

Front cover portraits *clockwise* David Bowie, Twiggy, Linford
Christie and Margaret Thatcher
Back cover portrait Yehudi Menuhin

PREFACE

'ONLY CONNECT...'

There was a moment in 1994 when photography took on a new meaning for me. I was at the funeral of a friend who had died too young. We weren't especially close, but we'd shared the warmth and respect of colleagues whose careers had collided briefly along their different trajectories. I'd come to know his wife, and had photographed the two of them with their children. We'd stayed in touch sporadically over the ensuing years.

On the day of his funeral, the mourners returned from church to his home for refreshments. I hadn't been there for several years, and as I moved from room to room, milling with the friends and relatives, I found myself face to face with the photographs I'd taken of him and his family, framed and hung all over the downstairs walls. Nothing more than blurry, playful snapshots of collapsing piggy-back rides and blond-haired, giggling boys and yet I found myself cast back not just to that sunny afternoon of the session, but to the specifics of our lives at that moment. The shiny faces were a reminder of the past but they were also, somehow, a distillation of the *relationships* that had united us at that moment.

Those pictures were about the lunch we'd had before taking them, and the tea we'd had just after; they were about the chatter of lives linked by work and hopes for the future, and the joking that knits the fabric of affection between people. They were about friendship. And I realised that despite the distance – geographically, in our ages, in our stages of life – my friend and I had stayed in touch over the years through these images. We were connected forever by the experience of that day, by the food and the sunshine and the laughter of the children. Through filtered light, in black and white, we had never really been apart.

Centurions, more than anything, is about keeping in touch – with a moment in time, with the history of a century, and with the people who have constituted that history. It's a way of drawing together some of the many people who have made up the backdrop of our lives at the end of an era.

It started out as an attempt to answer those idle wonderings that flit through all our minds on occasion, usually when we're immersed in other, 'more important' things; vague, fluttering thoughts that drift in-between plans and reminiscences and hover around the edges of daydreams, such as, I wonder whose idea it was to start The Samaritans?...Who came up with the notion of a hospice?...What do the people who discovered DNA actually look like?... Why Amnesty International and who started it?...How on earth can you make a baby in a test-tube and who first did it? ... Questions in response to the flash of a passing billboard, a news bulletin, an advertisement in the *Yellow Pages* opposite the page you were looking for, a discarded newspaper headline, somebody else's text book, a quick scan of titles in the wrong section of the bookshop...

Until one day it was no longer enough to wonder. It dawned on me that all those unknown faces belonged to people who had dramatically affected the quality of my life. It suddenly mattered to know who they were, to see what they looked like, to answer that basic, almost childish curiosity to put a face to the feat. I realised that all of them had inched civilisation forward in some way, had set the agenda, defined the tone, raised the stakes, set the standards against which we would be measured – had, in effect, established the boundaries of aspiration. As had a host of other, more 'media-celebrated' people in politics, the arts, the military, in industry, medicine and sport...

Centurions is a portrait of 100 ordinary people who, by virtue of their skill, vision, passion and drive, became *extraordinary*. They are the heroes of our grandparents and the inspiration for our children. They are the chubby schoolboys with scuffed knees who wanted to be train drivers, and the twirling ballerina girls who wanted to be Margot Fonteyn. They are all those dog-eared, faded photographs stuffed in suitcases in the attic. They are us, of course. And like us, they are part of history.

The following portraits are the results of conversations with people who have made a difference. They are a reflection of whatever connection was generated between us, the distillation of an engagement that was brief, fresh and tucked into hectic schedules. It was important to me to photograph these people as I found them – in the clothes they were in, in the light that contained them, where possible, and in the midst of our talk.

Photography, for me, is about relationships. Whether it is art or not, I wouldn't presume to know. But it is dialogue. And as such, to be shared.

CAROLYN DJANOGLY
July 1999

FOREWORD

Carolyn Djanogly sets out in this interesting and well-timed book to pay her own tribute to some of the many people who have left their impact on a century of change which is now drawing to a close.

It has been a distinctive century and this is a distinctive book. Change has been one of its major themes, change in ways of thinking and feeling as well as in ways of life, and many of the men and women Carolyn has selected have lived long enough to have experienced great changes in their own lives as well as in society. Behind each photograph there is an individual story.

One of the features of the overall national story has been that in the making of 20th-century history teams have been involved as well as individuals. Yet individuals have counted in this century, as in past centuries, with more of them than ever before making their own way, exploiting their talents, not their inheritance. They have shown drive in many different fields.

There is no standard 20th century type. Some of the characters featured are 'celebrities', a new word of this century, some are not. Some are linked with others in 'networks', another new word, some have worked alone. Most will be familiar, however, for the world is still a small place.

Centurions is very much Carolyn's project, conceived by her and carried through with vigour and imagination. Many of her subjects have been photographed often, for this has been a century of pictures more than words. Yet photographs capture people at different times and in different places, both in their own lives and in the life of the century. Carolyn has sought to distil the essence of these individuals by photographing them as they are, not as they could be 'set up' to be.

One of the most memorable books on the last century, the 19th, which is often compared with the 20th, whether we are historians or not, is G.M. Young's *Victorian England, Portrait of An Age*. It included no individual portraits, but as a historian, Young tried to capture what he called light and shade. Carolyn's is a whole portrait gallery in one volume, and through it we can capture much of the light and shade of our own century.

It has been very different from the 19th century and very different, too, from what people living at the end of the 19th century thought that it would be. Some trends, a favourite 20th-century word, have continued since then, some, like increased material wealth and greater longevity, we can trace back through our own century. Yet there have been many surprises. More and more information offered us has not eliminated them. Nor have computers.

Above all, there have been sharp contrasts within the span of the century – economic depression and economic affluence; 'total war', involving civilians as well as soldiers, sailors and airmen, and planned 'reconstruction'; horror, encapsulated in the Holocaust, and hope, sometimes expressed in political manifestos; science, offering both hope and apprehension, and superstition; religious zeal and total indifference; conservation and vandalism; natural as well as man-made disasters, and the effort genetically to control agriculture and animals. It has been a century of many themes and of many moods. Often the problems have dwarfed the opportunities.

In retrospect ours will stand out as the last century in a millennium, as it already is doing in its final decade. While it lasted, it was measured out in decades to which adjectives were applied ranging from 'bleak' to 'swinging'. The people Carolyn has photographed will doubtless have their own favourite decade or at least the decade which seemed to offer them the most. Yet their memories will gather around events and associations more than around decades, and the turning points in their own lives will not necessarily stand out as the turning points of the century.

The readers of this book will all have their own memories. Carolyn's photographs will doubtless refresh them. It is a pleasure as well as a privilege to introduce them.

ASA BRIGGS
April 1999

SPIKE MILLIGAN

Spike Milligan Hon.CBE
Born Terence Alan Milligan, 1918, Ahmadhagar, India

Spike Milligan is widely regarded as a comic genius, a writer and performer who has unleashed his unique and surreal brand of humour on the British public for over 50 years. Dubbed 'The Pied Piper of Nonsense' by *The Observer* newspaper, he is famous for his madcap antics on *The Goon Show*, his hilarious wartime memoirs and his affecting poetry.

The son of a gunner in the British Army based in India, Milligan enjoyed 15 years of colonial life before his family moved to London in 1933. After a series of dead-end jobs he joined the Harlem Club Band in Bexhill, singing and playing the trumpet. He served as an army gunner in North Africa and Italy during the Second World War, where he began to develop his particular skewed take on life, and entertained the troops with songs and sketches.

He made his television debut in the BBC show *Paging You* in 1947, his radio debut on *Opportunity Knocks* in 1949 and presented a children's comedy show, *The Junior Crazy Gang*, on the BBC Home Service in 1951. But it was his anarchic capers in *The Goon Show*, devised by him and performed with colleagues Peter Sellers, Harry Secombe and Michael Bentine, that propelled him to fame. A combination of innovative sketches and inspired clowning, it was a huge success, running from 1951-60, and has become a classic. Milligan won the TV Writer of the Year Award in 1956 for his series *A Show Called Fred* for Associated Rediffusion Television, and wrote and starred in his own television series, *Milligan at Large*, in 1963. He made the popular BBC 'Q' series between 1969 and 1980, and appeared in feature films such as *Alice's Adventures in Wonderland* (1972), *The Three Muskateers* (1973) and *Monty Python's Life of Brian* (1978).

He is the author of comic novels such as *Puckoon* (1963), humorous poetry and fiction for children, and auto-biographical works inspired by his wartime experiences, such as *Adolf Hitler, My Part In His Downfall* (1971), *Monty, His Part In My Victory* (1976) and *Where Have All The Bullets Gone?* (1985). In the 90s he began a series of comic rewrites of popular classics,...*According to Spike Milligan*, which include the re-telling of the *Bible* (1993), *Lady Chatterley's Lover* (1994) and *Black Beauty* (1996). Milligan was awarded the CBE in 1992 and the British Comedy Lifetime Achievement Award in 1994.

Pull the blinds
On your emotions
Switch off your face.
Put your love into neutral
This way to the human race.
From *Small Dreams of a Scorpion*, 1972

DAVID FROST

Sir David Frost OBE
Born 1939, Tenterden, Kent.

A pioneer of British television broadcasting, interviewer, producer and impresario David Frost has been a respected commentator on world events for the past 40 years. Esteemed for his incisive interviewing skills, which later coined the phrase 'trial by television', he is the only person to have interviewed the last six Presidents of the United States and the last six British Prime Ministers.

The son of a Methodist minister, Frost studied at Cambridge University, where he became an active member of *The Footlights Revue*, before starting his career in television as a trainee with the ITV company Associated Rediffusion in 1961. He came to prominence in 1962 as host and co-creator of the BBC's late-night satirical review programme *That Was The Week That Was* and won acclaim for *The Frost Report* (1966-67), an irreverent review of the weekly news, and *Frost on Friday* (1968-70), the hard-hitting current affairs programme.

The Frost Programme, a new style of programme broadcast from 1967-73, was the first current affairs show to 'grill' political figures in front of a live studio audience and pioneered the now ubiquitous programme format of audience participation. Awarded the double Emmy in America for *The David Frost Show* (1969-72), Frost began to establish a reputation as a formidable interrogator of world leaders with a series of landmark interviews, notably with US President Richard Nixon in 1976-7 and the late Shah of Iran, in exile, in 1980.

In 1983 he became joint founder of London Weekend Television and a year later was one of the team of four who launched TV-am, the first breakfast television programme. He presented *Frost on Sunday* for nine years before returning to the BBC in 1993 to present *Breakfast with Frost* on Sunday, which swiftly became the most influential political interview programme on British television, setting the agenda for the political week.

Frost has produced numerous television programmes, penned 15 books and produced eight films, including The *Slipper and The Rose* (1976) and the 1999 film *Rogue Trader*, about the life of Barings Bank fraudster Nick Leeson. Knighted in 1993, he has won all the major television awards, including the Golden Rose of Montreux, and continues to present *Breakfast with Frost*.

Bliss was it in that dawn to be alive, but to be young was very heaven...
From *The French Revolution*, by William Wordsworth, 1803

Main photograph: 18th October 1998, London
Inset photograph: Aged 9, in his back garden in Gillingham

DAVID HOCKNEY

David Hockney CH, RA
Born 1937, Bradford, Yorkshire

David Hockney is Britain's best-known modern artist,
whose broad body of work, from the exuberant Pop
Art paintings of the 1960s through line drawings,
photocollages and experiments with new media, has carried
him from the avant-garde to the mainstream, securing him
international acclaim en route and wielding enormous influence
in photography and advertising.

Hockney's artistic flair was apparent during his school days
when, as an active member of Bradford Grammar School art
club, he gained attention for his flamboyant posters advertising
school events. He studied at Bradford School of Art from 1953 to
1957, graduating with distinction, and enrolled at The Royal
College of Art in 1959.

He began to exhibit his work with other exponents of the
British Pop Art scene in the *Young Contemporaries* and *London
Group* exhibitions of 1960, where his bold colours and graffiti-
like figures drew critical attention. He lived in Los Angeles
during the mid-60s and developed his celebrated California
'swimming pool' paintings, such as *The Sunbather* (1966) and
A Bigger Splash (1967), studies of lean, tanned men lounging
around bright blue pools shimmering in the summer heat.
Painted with acrylics in electric colours, they were unveiled at his
solo exhibition in New York and remain some of his best-known
work. His later paintings were more representational and often
featured double portraits, such as the famous *Mr and Mrs Clark
and Percy* (1970).

In the early 70s Hockney diversified from heavy-colour
painting to fine-line drawing and print-making, and began
designing opera sets at the New York Metropolitan Opera and
at Glyndebourne. In the 80s his interest in Picasso and Cubism
led to explorations of perspective within photography and
printing, and in 1982 he exhibited detailed composite polaroids
and photocollages, composed from myriad separate shots, in
Drawing with a Camera in New York. In 1985 he was appointed
a Royal Academician, and in 1988 a major retrospective of his
work was mounted in Britain and America. The early 90s saw
his experimentation with computer technology, where faxes,
photocopies and digital ink-jet printings were employed to
produce works such as *The Studio March 28th 1996*, and in
1997 he was awarded the Companion of Honour.

In 1999 Hockney won the Royal Academy of Arts Charles
Wollaston Award for his series of monumental oil paintings, *A
Bigger Grand Canyon*.

They said, 'You have a blue guitar,
You do not play things as they are.'
The man replied, 'Things as they are
Are changed upon the blue guitar.'
From *The Man with the Blue Guitar*, by Wallace Stevens, 1936

Main photograph: 17th January 1999, West Kensington, London
Inset photograph: Aged 10, Bradford

JUDI DENCH

Dame Judi Dench
Born 1934, York

Judi Dench is one of Britain's most distinguished classical actresses, whose versatility has lent a magnetism to a diversity of roles from Shakespearean queens and the heroines of Greek tragedy to sensual and homely characters of contemporary theatre, film and television.

Dench was educated at a Quaker school and at the Central School of Speech and Drama in London, after which she joined the Old Vic Theatre Company in Liverpool and made her stage debut as Ophelia in *Hamlet* in 1957. She joined The Royal Shakespeare Company (RSC) in 1960 and the Nottingham Playhouse in 1961, and made her film debut in *The Third Secret* in 1964 and her television debut in the BBC series *Talking To A Stranger* in 1966. A spectacular performance as Sally Bowles in Hal Prince's London premiere of *Cabaret* in 1968 sealed her reputation as a leading theatrical talent and preceded a triumphant season with the RSC in 1976, where she played Lady Macbeth, Regan in *King Lear* and Adrianna in *The Comedy of Errors*.

Dench played a housewife opposite her real-life husband Michael Williams in the LWT sitcom *A Fine Romance* (1980-83) and established herself as an acclaimed character actress with her portrayal of Eleanor Lavish in the Merchant/Ivory film of E.M. Forster's book *A Room With A View* (1985) and Mrs Beaver in the film of Evelyn Waugh's book *A Handful of Dust* (1987). She won the Evening Standard Drama Award and the Olivier Award for her performance as Cleopatra in the National Theatre production of *Antony and Cleopatra* in 1987 and was awarded the DBE a year later. She made her directorial debut with a production of *Much Ado About Nothing* (1988) for Kenneth Brannagh's Renaissance Theatre Company, and in 1991 embarked on the first of six series of the hit BBC sitcom *As Time Goes By*.

Wooed by Hollywood, she was an enigmatic 'M' in the James Bond film *Goldeneye* (1995) and was nominated for an Academy Award for Best Actress for her stunning portrayal of a steely, yet vulnerable, Queen Victoria in John Madden's film *Mrs Brown* (1998). In 1999 Dench received the Oscar for Best Supporting Actress for her role as Queen Elizabeth I in Madden's hugely successful *Shakespeare in Love*, and her performance as an ageing actress in David Hare's play, *Amy's View*, which transferred from a successful British run in London's West End to a sell-out run on Broadway in the summer of 1999, was honoured by the Tony award for Best Actress.

'...there is a special providence in the fall of a sparrow. If it be now, 'tis not to come; if it be not to come, it will be now; if it be not now, yet it will come – the readiness is all.'
Hamlet, Act V, Scene II, *Hamlet*, by William Shakespeare

Main photograph: 10th June 1999, New York, USA
Inset photograph: Aged 4

RICHARD BRANSON

Richard Branson
Born 1950, Surrey

Entrepreneur Richard Branson is the founder and chairman of the Virgin Group, an internationally renowned £3 billion business conglomerate, whose brand name extends to almost every area of Britain's leisure and service industries. Famous for his outlandish publicity stunts, and dubbed the 'hippy capitalist', he has shunned conventional business practice, nurtured a pugnacious 'who dares wins' philosophy and been hailed as the spirit of free enterprise.

Branson's first venture was the launch of *Student* magazine in 1968, when he was just 16. He followed it two years later with the creation of Virgin, a mail-order record business that rapidly expanded to include a shop in London's Oxford Street in 1971. In 1972 he built a recording studio in Oxfordshire and recorded the first album on his Virgin label, *Tubular Bells* by Mike Oldfield, which was released a year later and went on to sell over five million copies. In the ensuing years the record stores multiplied, the Virgin label released albums by a variety of artists from the Rolling Stones to the Sex Pistols, and Megastores appeared throughout Britain and around the world.

Branson began to diversify Virgin's interests with the launch of a long-haul international airline, Virgin Atlantic Airways in 1984, and moved into the areas of computer games (1987), publishing (1991), radio (1993), soft drinks (1994), cinema (1995), the Internet and bridal services (1996) and financial services (1997). He sold Virgin Music Group to THORN-EMI for US$1billion in 1992 and increased his holdings in the travel industry with the purchase of two of Britain's rail franchises. While developing his businesses, he began to chase world speed records, achieving the fastest crossing of the Atlantic on his yacht, the Virgin Atlantic Challenger II, in 1985, and completing the first crossing of the Atlantic by balloon, accompanied by Per Lindstrand, two years later. In 1991 he broke the records for the longest flight by balloon (6,700 miles) and the fastest speed (up to 245 mph) crossing the Pacific Ocean, but was unsuccessful in his three attempts to circumnavigate the world.

Energetic and determined to have fun, Branson has built his business empire in his own image. Held up as a prototype for modern business practice, the Virgin story is much studied and its creator regarded as one of the most inspirational figures of our time.

You fail if you don't try.

Main photograph: 18th February 1999, Holland Park, London
Inset photograph: Aged 2, Devon

IAN BOTHAM

Ian Botham OBE
Born 1955, Heswall, Merseyside

A fearsome strike bowler, a batsman of awesome power and timing and an instinctive fielder, cricketer Ian Botham is widely acknowledged as England's greatest all-rounder, having chalked up a series of records in a spectacular 16-year career.

Tipped as a promising youngster during his school days, Botham joined Somerset cricket team in 1974, aged 19, and played county cricket until 1986. He made his debut in Test cricket in 1977 and quickly rose to prominence, taking his 100th wicket just two years later. In 1978, playing for England against Pakistan at Lords, he became the only player to score a century (108) and take eight wickets in an innings (8-34) in the same Test, and against India in 1980 he achieved an unrivalled Test double of a century and 13 wickets.

England captain for 12 Tests in 1980-81, Botham followed a disappointing season with the triumph of his career, winning the 1981 Test series against Australia almost single-handedly. In 1982, playing for England against India at Lord's, he made the fastest Test double century ever, and went on to win the BBC Sports Personality of the Year award.

Botham retired from Test cricket in 1992, having played for England in 102 matches, taken 383 wickets and scored 5,200 runs, and was awarded the OBE. He has completed numerous cross-country walks to raise funds for charity, notably journeying from John o'Groats to Land's End for the Leukaemia Research Fund and re-enacting Hannibal's crossing of the Alps, and commentated on cricket events for television. He will be remembered as one of the most charismatic, talented and influential sportsmen of our age.

'Life, Be in it'.

TONY BENN

The Rt. Hon. Tony Benn MP
Born Anthony Wedgwood Benn, 1925, London

Devout socialist, gifted orator, charismatic politician and Labour's longest-serving MP, Tony Benn is one of the most admired veterans of British politics. His turbulent 50-year career at Westminster has been dedicated to a single purpose, setting him at odds with politicians inside and out of his own party: the placing of greater power in the hands of the people.

The son of the Labour peer Viscount Stansgate, Benn served as a pilot in the RAF during the war before returning to New College, Oxford in 1945. Following a brief stint as a BBC producer, he began his political career in 1950 as the Labour MP for Bristol South-East, and was regarded then as a mainstream social democrat. In 1960 he inherited the title Viscount Stansgate and was consequently barred from sitting in the House of Commons. Refusing to use his title, he embarked on a famous three-year struggle, campaigning for the right of individuals to disclaim hereditary titles. The Peerage Act was finally passed in 1963 and Benn was re-elected MP for Bristol, regaining his seat in the House.

He held office in the Wilson and Callaghan administrations as Postmaster-General (1964-66), Minister of Technology (1966-70), Opposition Spokesman for Trade and Industry (1970-74) and, on Labour's return to government, Secretary of State for Industry (1974-75) before being transferred to the Department of Energy (1975-79) following his unsuccessful campaign against Britain's entry into the European Common Market. A member of Labour's national executive from 1959 to 1994, and chairman of the party in 1971, Benn mounted the main left-wing challenge to the Labour leadership, standing unsuccessfully in the 1976 and 1987 elections. He refused a place in the shadow cabinet in 1979 and was narrowly defeated in his bid for the deputy leadership in 1981 by Denis Healey. Following the abolition of his Bristol constituency in 1983, he returned to Parliament in 1984 as MP for Chesterfield.

An inveterate anti-war campaigner, with a firm belief in examining the past for insights into the political present, Benn has written several books, including Arguments for Socialism (1979) and Arguments for Democracy (1981), and published seven volumes of his detailed diaries, started when a schoolboy, which have become a substantial personal and political archive.

'Dare to be a Daniel.
Dare to stand alone.
Dare to have a purpose firm.
Dare to let it be known.'
Advice to the young Tony from his father

Main photograph: 28th July 1998, Holland Park, London
Inset photograph: Aged 6, in the Tower Gardens, Westminster

TERENCE CONRAN

Sir Terence Conran
Born 1931, Surrey

Terence Conran is the designer and entrepreneur who has successfully persuaded post-war Britain to embrace Mediterranean cooking, recline on modern furniture and sleep under a duvet.

Conran studied textile design at the Central School of Arts and Crafts in London before setting up his own furniture-making business in 1952, aged 21. His love of good food was inspired by a trip to France in 1953, where he briefly worked in a Paris restaurant, before returning home to open The Soup Kitchen, off Trafalgar Square.

His ventures in design and retailing in the 1950s, 60s and 70s made him a household name. In 1956 he founded the Conran Design Group, which became one of the biggest design consultancies in the world. In 1964 he broke into the retail trade with the opening of the first Habitat store in London's Fulham Road, which offered a combination of his own designs, functional furniture and classic French cookware. By 1980 there were 47 Habitat stores in the UK, as well as stores throughout France, the USA and Japan, and an up-market sister company in London, The Conran Shop, which sold exclusive home furnishings. Knighted in 1983, Conran extended his interests, establishing the Next chains and merging Habitat with retailers such as Mothercare, Heal's, Richard Shops and British Home Stores to form the multi-million pound Storehouse Group in 1986.

In 1987 he opened Bibendum in Fulham Road, rekindling his love affair with the restaurant business, and went on to open a further 21 restaurants and bars in London, including Le Pont de la Tour, Quaglino's, Bluebird and Sartoria, and one in Paris, Alcazar. Throughout the 90s he expanded his restuarant and retail interests and designed Conran Collection, an exclusive range of houseware products. The recipient of numerous awards, including the D&AD President's Award for Outstanding Contribution to British Design, Conran was appointed Commandeur des Arts et des Lettres in 1992. He has published a variety of books about interior design, cookery and gardening.

I'm in business largely because of personal pleasure. I like the things I do. The restaurants, the shops, the books......they are my golf courses.

Main photograph: 11th May 1998, London
Inset photograph: Aged 10

SIMON RATTLE

Sir Simon Rattle CBE
Born 1955, Liverpool

Conductor Simon Rattle is the dynamic, young musical talent who has transformed the perception of classical music in Britain. Famous for raising the City of Birmigham Symphony Orchestra (CBSO) to international distinction, he has revitalised the classics, championed contemporary British composers, such as Harrison Birtwistle and Thomas Adès, and attracted a wider audience to both.

An accomplished child pianist, Rattle began playing percussion with the Merseyside Youth Orchestra at the age of 10, before studying the art of conducting at the Royal Academy of Music in London. He made his professional debut with the Philharmonia Orchestra at the London Festival Hall in 1976 and, a year later, joined the BBC Scottish Symphony Orchestra as Assistant Conductor, making his Glyndebourne premiere with Janacek's *The Cunning Little Vixen*. He became Associate Conductor of the Liverpool Philharmonic, and in 1980 was appointed Principal Conductor of the CBSO at the startlingly youthful age of 25. Following spectacular performances of Mahler's 10th Symphony, he dramatically reversed the fortunes of the ailing Midlands orchestra by rejuvenating its repertoire with a dazzling programme of modern classical music combined with more traditional fare.

In the 1980s Rattle collaborated with numerous orchestras worldwide and was Artistic Director of the Aldeburgh Festival from 1982 to 1993. Awarded the CBE in 1987, he was appointed Music Director of the CBSO in 1990, and was instrumental in the creation of the Birmingham Symphony Hall, now hailed as one of the world's finest auditoria. In 1991 he launched *Towards the Millennium*, a decade-long retrospective of 20th-century music, and became Principal Guest Conductor with the Orchestra of the Age of Enlightenment, conducting sell-out productions of Mozart's *Cosi Fan Tutte* (1991) and *Don Giovanni* (1994). Knighted in 1994, he produced *Leaving Home* in 1996, a BAFTA-award winning Channel 4 television series on 20th-century orchestra music.

One of EMI's most successful artists, Rattle has made more than 60 award-winning recordings, including *Mahler 2*, *Porgy and Bess*, and *Szymanowski Violin Concertos 1 & 2*. Since departing the CBSO in 1998 he has achieved international acclaim for his work with the leading symphony orchestras of Vienna and North America, and in June 1999 he was appointed Music Director of the Berlin Philharmonic Orchestra, for commencement in 2002.

All before. Nothing else ever. Ever tried. Ever failed. No matter. Try again. Fail again. Fail better.
From *Worstward Ho*, by Samuel Beckett, 1981

GERMAINE GREER

Professor Greer
Born 1939, Melbourne, Australia

Writer, feminist and academic, Germaine Greer is the author of one of the most revolutionary texts of the 20th century, *The Female Eunuch*. Published in 1970, it controversially portrayed marriage as a legalised form of slavery for women, attacked the denial and misrepresentation of female sexuality by a male-dominated society, and issued a clarion call for the immediate empowerment of women. It caused an explosion in sexual politics and sold over a million copies worldwide.

Greer worked as Senior Tutor in English at Sydney University before coming to Britain in 1964 on a scholarship to Cambridge University, where she completed her Ph.D. She became a lecturer in English at Warwick University (1967-72) and emerged as an outspoken feminist, writing for a variety of periodicals including the underground magazine *Oz*. In 1970, with the publication of what became known as the 'feminists' bible', *The Female Eunuch*, she was propelled into the vanguard of discussion of women's liberation and took the helm with characteristic boldness. Throughout the 70s she worked as a freelance writer and journalist, and published *The Obstacle Race* (1979), an examination of the lives and work of female painters.

Greer founded, and became director of, the Tulsa Center for the Study of Women's Literature in Oklahoma in 1979. She published several books in the 80s, including *Sex and Destiny: The Politics of Human Fertility* (1984), and became a lecturer at Newnham College, Cambridge in 1989. In 1991 she published *The Change*, a frank and thorough examination of women, ageing and the menopause. She returned to Warwick University as Professor of English and Comparative Studies in 1997, and in 1999 published *The Whole Woman*, the sequel to *The Female Eunuch*. Arguing that women have long been damaged by the pressure to conform to a male-designated ideal of femininity, she criticises feminists' prevailing tendency to be sidetracked by the quest for *equality* with men above personal liberation.

Revered for her formidable intellect, Greer's impact on the lives of post-war women has been, and continues to be, immense.

A woman who cannot organise her sex life to her best advantage is hardly likely to transform society.

DAVID BAILEY

David Bailey FRPS, FCSD
Born 1938, Leytonstone, London

One of Britain's leading photographers, David Bailey burst out of the East End in the early 1960s and revolutionised fashion, portrait and documentary photography. Celebrated for his iconic images of the fashionable and notorious elite at the helm of the 'Swinging Sixties', from 'The Shrimp' and Twiggy to Warhol and the Kray twins, he has continued to define the spirit of the decades with a diverse body of anthropological and documentary portraiture.

After national service with the RAF, Bailey assisted top London photographer John French in 1958, and two years later, aged just 21, shot his first cover for *Vogue*. He rapidly established a reputation for striking, high-contrast studio portraiture, creating luminous studies of doe-eyed beauties of the day, such as Jean Shrimpton, Penelope Tree and Catherine Deneuve. One of the first fashion photographers to use a 35mm camera, he liberated his models from the confines of the studio and set them against the gritty, urban backdrop of London and New York, producing work of spontaneity and irreverence which, coupled with a hard-edged realism, came to epitomise the cool new urban glamour of the times.

Bailey published his first book, *Box of Pin-Ups*, a chronicle of celebrity friends such as Michael Caine and The Beatles, in 1964, and from 1968 began directing television commercials and documentaries. His photographic tribute to the 60s, *Goodbye, Baby, Amen*, was published in 1969 and his later diversification into reportage was reflected in the books *Beady Minces* (1974), a selection of snapshots of people from around the world, and *Another Image: Papua New Guinea* (1975). Numerous exhibitions of his work were held throughout the 80s, including a retrospective at the Victoria & Albert Museum in 1983, and he published a range of books, such as *Trouble and Strife* (1980), *Nudes 1981-84* (1984) and *David Bailey's London NW1* (1982). He has continued to direct films and drama throughout the 90s and to publish several more collections of work, including a tribute to his wife, Catherine Dyer, in *The Lady is a Tramp* (1995).

Bailey's exhibition *The Birth of the Cool* was held at The Barbican Art Gallery in April 1999.

I don't have a style. I'm interested in the person, always was.

JOHN LE CARRÉ

John Le Carré
Born David Cornwell, 1931, Poole, Dorset

John Le Carré, the pen name adopted by the writer David Cornwell, has been described as the greatest fictional spymaster of all time. Celebrated for his masterly depiction of betrayal and subterfuge in the post-Second World War era, his is an intricately crafted, prolific and hugely popular output.

Educated at Berne and Oxford universities, Le Carré undertook his military service in the Intelligence Corps and was posted to Austria before studying modern languages at Lincoln College, Oxford. He became assistant master at Eton before joining the British Foreign Service in 1959, working in Germany. Stimulated by his five years' experience of the shady world of diplomacy and espionage, and inspired by the intrigues and paranoia generated by the Cold War, he wrote a detective story, *Call for The Dead*, which was published in 1961, and introduced the secret world of his anti-hero George Smiley, who was to feature in several later works. In 1962 he produced *A Murder of Quality*, but shot to international fame in 1963 with his highly acclaimed novel *The Spy Who Came In From The Cold*, which has since sold more than 20 million copies.

Le Carré left the British Foreign Service in 1963 to write full-time. *The Looking Glass War* was published in 1965, followed by *A Small Town In Germany* in 1968. He briefly moved away from espionage territory with his 1971 novel *The Naïve and Sentimental Lover*, but returned with the trilogy *Tinker, Tailor, Soldier, Spy* (1974), *The Honourable Schoolboy* (1977) and *Smiley's People* (1980). *The Little Drummer Girl* followed in 1983, and his most autobiographical novel, *A Perfect Spy* (1986) preceded *The Russia House* in 1989. Smiley took his final bow in *The Secret Pilgrim* (1992), leaving critics predicting a paralysis of Le Carré's imaginary powers after the end of the Cold War. He proved them wrong with three best-selling novels, *The Night Manager* (1993), *Our Game* (1995) and *The Tailor of Panama* (1996), in which powerful governments, international corporations and organised crime compete for supremacy.

Le Carré's fiction has earned him many literary awards, including the James Tait Black Memorial Prize, the Crime Writers' Association Gold Dagger and the Somerset Maugham Award for *The Honourable Schoolboy*. His work has inspired several film and television adaptations, most memorably the immortalisation of Smiley by Sir Alec Guinness in the 1982 BBC series of *Smiley's People*. His 17th novel, *Single and Single*, was published in 1999.

'A man is judged by what he looks for, not by what he finds.'
Cassidy, in Le Carré's *The Naïve and Sentimental Lover*, 1971

Main photograph: 26th May 1998, Hampstead, London
Inset photograph: Aged 8

VERA LYNN

Dame Vera Lynn
Born Vera Welch, 1917, London

The 'Forces' Sweetheart', Vera Lynn was one of the most celebrated singers of the 1940s and 50s. Her searing renditions of patriotic songs, such as *We'll Meet Again* and *White Cliffs of Dover*, performed in the war zones of Europe, rallied the spirits of British servicemen during World War Two and endeared her to the nation forever.

Making her debut in 1924, aged just seven, Lynn sang in working-men's clubs before joining a juvenile troupe known as Madame Harris's Kracker Kabaret Kids in 1928. In 1931 she became a band singer with Howard Baker, before making her first radio broadcast in 1935 with the Joe Loss Orchestra. Later that year she joined the Charlie Kunz band and cut her first record, *I'm in the Mood For Love*, after which she joined the Ambrose Orchestra in 1937 and had her first hit, *The Little Boy That Santa Claus Forgot*. In 1939 she was voted the most popular singer in Britain in a newspaper competition and became the British troops' favourite pin-up.

Lynn went solo in 1941 and performed in the *Apple Sauce* revue at the London Palladium before becoming a household name with her successful radio show, *Sincerely Yours*, which ran for six years and provided a vital link with home for servicemen overseas. By now Britain's biggest singing star, she toured Europe, entertaining troops with a series of sentimental wartime ballads delivered in her striking, melodious voice. In 1952 she became the first British artist to top both British and American charts with *Auf Wiedersehen Sweetheart*, following it with hits such as *Forget Me Not* (1952) and *My Son, My Son* (1954), and embarked on her long-running Radio Luxembourg series, *Vera Lynn Sings*. Recording, touring and hosting television specials throughout the 1960s, she was a regular guest at soldiers' reunions throughout the 70s and 80s.

Honoured for her music and her humanitarian work, Lynn has performed in seven Royal Command Performances and achieved fourteen gold records in her career. Regarded as a national institution, she was awarded the DBE in 1975 and gave a special concert in 1994 to commemorate the 50th anniversary of the D-Day landings.

'The Second World War was started by Vera Lynn's agent,' some comic cracked in the early seventies. A writer said: 'During the war years, Vera had History working for her as an agent.' They were two ways of expressing the same thing: that what I was doing, and the way I was doing it, just happened to be right for the time. And everything was right, even down to what we've since learned to call the media. When families and sometimes whole populations are scattered by war, the great uniting link is radio, while the simplest, most portable form of instant entertainment at that time was the gramophone record and the wind-up gramophone. Broadcasting and recording were my natural outlets; songs that spoke for very ordinary people were my chosen means of expression.

RICHARD DAWKINS

Professor Dawkins
Born 1941, Nairobi, Kenya

The zoologist and evolutionary biologist Richard Dawkins is the ardent Darwinian whose passion for the natural world and scientific truth has opened up the frontiers of science to a mass audience through his best-selling publications. Celebrated for his skilful ability to explain scientific discoveries and hypotheses in laymen's terms, he has had a significant impact on the way we regard 'life, the universe and everything.'

Dawkins left Africa for England at the age of eight and was educated at Oxford University, where he gained his doctorate in zoology in 1966 and became a lecturer. In 1976 his career as a celebrity scientist was launched with the publication of his first, and perhaps best known, book, *The Selfish Gene*, in which he proposed the idea that humans are fundamentally 'temporary survival machines' who are programmed by 'selfish' genes to propagate themselves. He provoked further controversy by asserting that seemingly altruistic behaviour in animals and humans was simply a strategy to ensure their ongoing survival. The compelling first person narrative, clear descriptions and colourful metaphors ensured instant accessibility, and the book became a cult text.

Dawkins elaborated on his neo-Darwinist ideas in most of his following books. *The Extended Phenotype* (1982) discussed the effect genes can have on organisms outside of the body and *The Blind Watchmaker* (1986) explained how cumulative selection of numerous small genetic changes can transform simple features into more complex organs. *River Out of Eden* (1995) offered further proof of the validity of evolutionary theory and *Climbing Mount Improbable* (1996) is a collection of evolutionary tales covering the beauty of spiders' webs to the origins of flight.

Appointed Oxford University's first Charles Simonyi Professor of Public Understanding of Science in 1995 and elected a Fellow of the Royal Society of Literature in 1997, Dawkins published *Unweaving the Rainbow* in 1998. An impassioned and provocative defence of scientific exploration against the charge that it undermines the poetic imagination, he argues that the truth revealed through the clarity of science greatly enhances our appreciation of its beauty.

After sleeping through a hundred million centuries we have finally opened our eyes on a sumptuous planet, sparkling with colour, bountiful with life. Within decades we must close our eyes again. Isn't it a noble, an enlightened way of spending our brief time in the sun, to work at understanding the universe and how we have come to wake up in it?
From *Unweaving the Rainbow*, by Dawkins, 1998

Main photograph: 31st June 1998, Oxford
Inset photograph: Aged 8

STANLEY MATTHEWS

Sir Stanley Matthews CBE
Born 1915, Stoke-on-Trent

Legendary footballer Stanley Matthews, 'The Wizard of
Dribble', was born to 'The Fighting Barber of Hanley',
the formidable featherweight boxer Jack Matthews, from
whom the young Stanley inherited a life-long dedication to
fitness.

Arguably the finest exponent of wing artistry football has
ever seen, Matthews practised his unique footballing skills as a
child, dribbling an inflated pig's bladder in the streets of Stoke,
by gas lamp. He began playing semi-professional soccer at the
age of 14, joining his local side, Stoke City, in 1931 and, in a career
spanning 33 years played in 886 first class matches, attaining 54
international caps. During World War Two he served as a PT
instructor in the RAF, before transferring to Blackpool Football
Club in 1947, where he remained until 1961.

A superb stylist who excelled at eluding the opposition,
Matthew's mesmerising skills brought adoring crowds to their
feet wherever he played. Voted the first ever Footballer of the
Year in 1948 by the Football Writers' Association, he won the FA
Cupwinner's medal in 1953, aged 38, and became the oldest
player ever to perform in the First Division, five days after his
fiftieth birthday in February 1965. He retired at the end of the
season and became the first professional footballer to receive a
knighthood.

Hailed as football's first international superstar, Matthews
is regarded as a national hero and ambassador for Britain, the
country which gave football to the world. Part of the inscription
on the mounting of the statue erected in his honour in Stoke in
1987 outlines his legacy – 'a magical player, of the people, for the
people.'

Memories are the things I treasure, not medals and honours. The
memory of that hour in the dressing–room before kick-off, when
you prepared yourself for the game ahead. I always had a shower
and a massage, then I was physically sick. Every Saturday,
almost without fail for 33 years, that's how nervous I was. But it's
a wonderful feeling, that kind of excitement....

Main photograph: 25th March 1997, Stoke-on-Trent
Inset photograph: Aged 10

NORMAN FOSTER

Lord Foster OM, RA, RIBA
Born 1935, Redditch, Manchester

Master architect Norman Foster has dotted the skylines of the world's major cities with his trademark light-filled, steel and glass edifices. A leading exponent of hi-tech architecture, his aerodynamic designs articulate a consistent and elegant vision of the modern age.

Foster studied architecture and city planning at Manchester University before winning a scholarship to Yale University in 1961, where he met British architect Richard Rogers. In 1963 they teamed up with Su Rogers and Wendy Cheesman in a London-based practice called Team 4, and rose to prominence in 1965 with their innovative design for the Reliance Controls building in Swindon.

Foster set up Foster Associates in 1967 when Team 4 disbanded, and established a reputation as one of Britain's most talented and visionary architects with his design for the Willis Faber Dumas Building in Ipswich in 1975, a sleek, black glass-walled office block that has since become a Grade 1 listed building. The Sainsbury Centre for Visual Arts at the University of East Anglia and IBM's Technical Park in Middlesex followed in 1977 and 1979 respectively, but it was his design for the Hong Kong and Shanghai Bank, a hi-tech monument of steel and glass which, at the time, was the world's most expensive building, which propelled him to international celebrity. Knighted in 1990, he completed Century Tower in Tokyo, the world's highest skyscraper, in 1991 as well as the ITN headquarters in London and a new, airy terminal at Stansted Airport.

In 1992 Foster founded Foster and Partners and completed his communications tower for the Barcelona Olympics. A year later, he finished the Carré d'Art Gallerie Médiathèque in Nîmes, France. In 1998 he oversaw the completion of two epic productions, the mammoth Chek Lap Kok airport, a vast, vaulted, steel-covered terminal built on an artificial island south of Hong Kong, and the renovation of the Berlin Reichstag, inside whose shell he created a dramatic 'cathedral of glass'. In 1999 he continued working on the 92-storey Millennium Tower, which will replace the bomb-damaged Baltic Exchange in London, and collaborated with sculptor Anthony Caro on the design of a new Thames pedestrian bridge, due for completion in 2000.

Foster was made a Life Peer in June 1999.

Architecture is a very down-to-earth business. People have a building because they need it. It's like the bar stool. You only design the bar stool because you don't want to stand up. It's not because somebody says, 'Hey, let's do a wonderful act of philanthropy.' The final test is when you compare your bar stool with everybody else's. Yours has to look the best, feel the most comfortable and cost a fraction of the others.

Main photograph: 20th October 1998, London
Inset photograph: Aged 18 months

BOB GELDOF

Bob Geldof Hon.KBE
Born 1954, Dublin

Bob Geldof is the rock singer turned humanitarian whose co-ordination of Band Aid and Live Aid in the mid-1980s harnessed the talents of the biggest names in the world of pop music, stirred the conscience of the nation, raised over £120 million for famine relief in Africa and spawned a plethora of charity records and aid projects.

Educated by Jesuits at Blackrock College, Dublin, Geldof moved to Canada in his early twenties to pursue his passion for music and workrd as a pop journalist. Keen to make his mark on the burgeoning punk rock scene, he returned to Ireland in 1975 and formed the rock band The Boomtown Rats. Playing a mixture of R&B and punk music, they were signed to the Ensign record label in 1977 and produced eight hits in the following three years, including two Number Ones with *Rat Trap* (1978) and *I Don't Like Mondays* (1979). In the early 80s Geldof began to pursue a solo career, and made his screen debut in Alan Parker's film of the Pink Floyd album, *The Wall*, in 1982.

In 1984, deeply affected by television images of famine in Ethiopia, Geldof persuaded fellow musicians to record the first charity single by an all-star rock group, which he named Band Aid. *Do They Know It's Christmas?*, written by Geldof and Midge Ure, became the biggest-selling UK single and raised £8 million for famine relief. The success inspired him to orchestrate Live Aid, the most ambitious rock concert ever, which divided into two marathon concerts, staged simultaneously in London and Philadelphia on 13th July 1985, which were broadcast by satellite to an estimated one billion viewers world-wide and raised over £50 million.

Geldof was awarded an honorary knighthood in 1986 and numerous other accolades for his charity extravaganzas, including the UN World Hunger Award, and was nominated three times for the Nobel Peace Prize. He released two solo albums between 1986 and 1988, and moved into producing, co-founding the multi-award winning Planet 24 radio and television production company in 1992. He remains Chairman of the Band Aid Trust.

I'm for thinking
Between the ears
For mental process
For cogs and gears
I'm for flesh
And I'm for mind
I'm for people
I'm for life.
From the song *A Hold of Me*, by Geldof, 1984

Main photograph: 23rd October 1998, London
Inset photograph: Aged 13, Dublin

ROBERT EDWARDS

Professor Robert Edwards CBE, FRS
Born 1925, Batley, Yorkshire

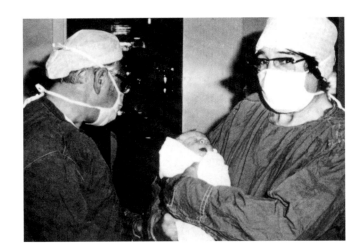

Robert Edwards is the pioneering scientist who, in collaboration with the late gynaecologist Dr Patrick Steptoe, introduced in-vitro fertilisation (IVF) for the treatment of infertility and genetic disease in human embryos, one of the most significant medical and scientific breakthroughs of the century, which resulted in the birth of the world's first 'test-tube' baby, Louise Brown, on 26th July 1978.

Edwards trained in mammalian embryology and genetics, studying mouse embryology in the mid-1950s, and worked as a scientist at the California Institute of Technology, the National Institute of Medical Research in London and at Glasgow University before joining the Department of Physiology at Cambridge University in 1964.

Following his success with in-vitro fertilisation of mice, he wanted to apply his findings clinically, and in 1968 he met gynaecologist Patrick Steptoe, later president of the British Fertility Society, who shared his belief in the potential benefits of such a mission. Despite vociferous objections about the moral and ethical implications of their study, the two embarked on their work from Steptoe's base at the John Kershaw Cottage Hospital in Oldham.

They recruited 400 infertile couples in the early 1970s. Steptoe extracted eggs from a number of the women, using laperoscopy, and Edwards fertilised them with their husbands' sperm in a culture dish. Newly formed embryos were then re-planted in the womb, but the women failed to become pregnant. Steptoe and Edward altered the treatment, developing methods of ovarian stimulation to produce more than one egg for collection and modifying the technique of prescribing fertility drugs to the women to work with the one, naturally ovulating egg. As a result, Leslie Brown, a 30-year-old housewife from Bristol, carried to term and delivered a healthy 5lb 12 oz baby girl.

Their achievement heralded a new era of hope for infertile women and led to dramatic advances in the field of reproductive science. They established the world's largest IVF clinic at Bourn Hall, Cambridge in 1980, and Edwards founded the European Society of Human Reproduction and Embryology in 1984. Awarded the CBE in 1988, Edwards is currently editor of three journals on reproductive issues.

Within five seconds, ten seconds of birth, she let out the biggest yell you've ever heard a baby cry and Patrick shouted out, "That's what I like to hear, good lung development!" and everything was wonderful.....It was astonishing. It was hope to thousands and thousands of patients, and for us, it was the end of a very long and difficult story. It had taken 16 years and now we had a baby, a beautiful baby. A new future was opening....
On the birth of Louise Brown, the first 'test-tube' baby.

Main photograph: 17th October 1998, Cambridge
Inset photograph: Edwards holding baby Louise Brown, with Steptoe

STIRLING MOSS

Stirling Moss OBE
Born 1929, London

Charismatic daredevil Stirling Moss achieved cult status in the 1950s and early 60s as the driver who dominated British motor racing, winning 16 Grand Prix trophies and achieving second place in four Formula One championships.

Moss began his career in 1948, aged 19, driving a Cooper 500, and joined Peter Heath's HWM team in 1950, in whose cars he achieved his first international success. He drove a variety of cars from 1952 onwards, including Coopers and a Maserati in the Grands Prix, as well as Jaguars in sports car events, and briefly joined the Maserati works team in 1954.

In 1955 he switched to Mercedes-Benz for what was to become the most triumphant year of his career. Clocking up a second place in the Drivers' Championship, Moss went on to win his first British Grand Prix and the gruelling Mille Miglia and Targa Floria events, driving a Mercedes 300 SLR sports car. In 1956 he rejoined Maserati, clinching another second place in the Drivers' Championship, and a year later won his second British Grand Prix. Driving for Vanwall in 1957 and 1958, he was again runner-up in the Drivers' Championship, losing by a single point in 1958, but teamed up with Jack Brabham the same year to win the Nurburgring 1000 km race in an Aston Martin sports car, winning the event again in 1959.

Further Formula One successes followed in the Lotus and Cooper cars for the Rob Walker team until 1960, when Moss broke both legs in a dramatic crash at Spa in Belgium. Despite a remarkable come-back in the same year, he decided to retire in 1962 after another serious crash, this time in a Formula Two race at Goodwood. He went on to establish a career as a motorsports journalist and broadcaster, and returned to saloon car racing in 1980.

Feted as one of the most inspiring ambassadors of his sport, Moss's reputation for risk-taking and his passion for winning are legendary. The World Championship may have eluded him, but his fearlessness and flair behind the wheel have earned him a place in popular culture that extends well beyond the race track. As anyone who has ever jumped a light or been caught speeding will know, 'Who do you think you are, Stirling Moss?' has become a classic rebuke.

I didn't drive just because I liked going fast. I drove because I loved the competition– the competition of trying to beat another man. Also, the competition between myself and the car. I would rather lose a race driving fast enough to win, than win one driving slow enough to lose it! A crazy philosophy, but a great passion.

Main photograph: 23rd March 1998, London
Inset photograph: Aged 10

GILBERT & GEORGE

Gilbert – Born 1943, Dolomites, Italy
George – Born 1942, Devon

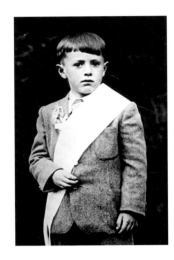

Gilbert and George are two – or possibly one – of Britain's best known artists, a double-act who, having adopted a fused persona known as 'G&G', have presented themselves as 'Living Sculpture' for over 30 years. Flagrant self-publicists, renowned for their lurid photopieces featuring magnified samples of bodily excreta, they have been the recipients of the Turner Prize and a wealth of adulation and disgust.

Gilbert, the son of a shoe-maker, began making wood carvings as a teenager, studying at the Munich Academy of Art before moving to London in 1965. George took painting classes at Dartington Hall in Totnes and studied at Oxford School of Art. They met as students in 1967 at St Martin's School of Art in London, experiencing 'love at first sight', and became inseparable. Evolving the theory that an artist could exist without a gallery, they declared *themselves* the work of art, and have dedicated their lives to its perpetual display. Donning identical, single-breasted, worsted suits that have become their uniform, they first demonstrated their concept with the legendary 'Singing Sculpture' in 1968, whereby they stood on a table in a gallery, faces daubed with metallic paint, one holding a cane, the other rubber gloves, and sang *Underneath the Arches* without pause, for an eight-hour period.

G&G began subjecting the most rudimentary aspects of their daily lives, such as walking and eating, to their particular brand of scrutiny, and packaging them into artworks. Their sculptures and photopieces, such as the 1970 collage of portraits of themselves laughing, labelled *George the Cunt* and *Gilbert the Shit* (1970), were clearly designed to tempt, mock, shock and threaten, and subsequent productions have included *Paki* (1978), featuring the artists on either side of a young Asian man, *Sperm Eaters* (1982), *Holy Cock* (1982) and *Friendship Pissing* (1983).

In 1986 they won the Turner Prize for a series of acclaimed exhibitions in New York and Europe, which featured works entitled *Flower Worship* (1982) and *Coming* (1983).

Disciplined and prolific, self-confessedly apolitical and opinionless, their 'Art for All' includes *The Naked Shit Pictures* (1994) and *The New Testamental Pictures* (1998), the latter depicting images of the artists and magnified drops of urine, blood, semen and tears. Whilst contentious subject matter and consciously eccentric behaviour have guaranteed Gilbert and George notoriety, their unique vision has contributed to the merging of traditional distinctions between painting, sculpture and performance, and inspired a generation of new artists.

We are only human sculptors in that we get up every day, walking sometimes, reading rarely, eating often, thinking always, smoking moderately, enjoying enjoyment, looking, relaxing to see, loving nightly, finding amusement, encouraging life, fighting boredom, being natural, daydreaming, travelling along, drawing occasionally, talking lightly, tea drinking, feeling tired, dancing sometimes, philosophising a lot, criticising never, whistling tunefully, dying very slowly, laughing nervously, greeting politely and waiting 'til the day breaks.

Main photograph: 8th September 1998, Fournier Street, East London
Inset photographs: Gilbert, aged 5; George, aged 7

DORIS LESSING

Doris Lessing
Born 1919, Kermanshah, Iran

Doris Lessing is one of the most original and prolific of contemporary writers, who rose to literary prominence in the 1950s with a socially-charged brand of fiction which challenged prevailing notions of nationality, identity and sexuality. A writer of immense scope, she has applied a fierce and questioning intelligence to her own life, and to the experience of colonial existence in her native Africa, producing some of the most controversial and thought-provoking writing of our time.

A farmer's daughter, Lessing was brought up in Southern Rhodesia from the age of five, and moved to Salisbury in 1937, where she first became involved in politics and helped to found a non-racist, left-wing party. After two brief marriages, she came to London in 1949, aged 30, and a year later, published her first novel, *The Grass is Singing*, a critique of white civilisation in Africa, which met with instant acclaim.

She published *Martha Quest* in 1952, the first of five novels in a partly autobiographical sequence, *The Children of Violence*, which focuses on issues of social and psychological change, and during this time briefly joined the Communist Party. In 1954 she won the Somerset Maugham Award for her collection of short novels called *Five*, but it was the publication of *The Golden Notebook* in 1963, which questioned beliefs about self, sexuality, authority and the confines of the imaginative life, that confirmed her status as one of the most significant post-war novelists.

In 1971 Lessing published *Briefing for a Descent into Hell*, a fictional study of so-called mental breakdown, and went on to explore her social and philosophical preoccupations in a quintet of space-fiction novels called *Canopus in Argos: Archives* (1979-83). In 1985 *The Good Terrorist* netted the W.H.Smith Literary Award, and the first volume of her autobiography, *Under My Skin*, won the James Tait Black Memorial Prize and the L.A.Times Book Prize in 1994. The second volume, *Walking in the Shade*, followed in 1997. Three times shortlisted for the Booker Prize, and with an array of short stories, non-fiction, plays and poetry to her name, Lessing published her 22nd novel, *Mara and Dann*, in 1999.

I do find the world less and less convincing as I get older. It's such a dream and a shadow as it rushes past. I do think there is something else...

EDWARD HEATH

The Rt. Hon. Sir Edward Heath MBE, MP
Born 1916, Broadstairs, Kent

The 'Father of the House of Commons', Edward Heath is the longest-serving Member of Parliament and the former Conservative Prime Minister who successfully guided Britain into the European Economic Community.

The son of a carpenter, Heath studied music at Balliol College, Oxford, and after serving in the British Army during World War Two, briefly worked as a journalist and banker before being elected to Parliament as the Conservative MP for Old Bexley and Sidcup in 1950. In 1955 he became chief whip in Winston Churchill's government and then Minister of Labour in 1959 under Harold Macmillan. From 1960-63, he was Lord Privy Seal with foreign office responsibilities, and during this time he served as chief negotiator for Britain's unsuccessful bid to enter the European Common Market.

In 1963 he became Secretary of State for Industry, Trade and Regional Development until the government's defeat in the 1964 election. A year later he replaced Sir Alec Douglas-Home as Conservative leader and steered his party to victory in the 1970 General Election. He went on to achieve his greatest political feat with the signing of the historic Treaty of Accession in Brussels in January 1972, which took Britain into the EEC. At home, Heath maintained a domestic policy that shunned direct intervention in the economy and resulted in widespread strikes and a steep rise in unemployment. He was forced into a U-turn to counteract the situation, and although a brief period of reflation followed, further strikes and a long, stand-off battle with the miners ensued, leading to the three-day week and electoral defeat in 1974. A year later he was ousted as leader by Margaret Thatcher and returned to the backbenches.

Heath has remained an influential figure in foreign affairs, participating in negotiations with Saddam Hussein for the release of hostages on the eve of the 1991 Gulf War and attending the handover of Hong Kong in 1997, in recognition of his longstanding diplomatic relations with China.

Knighted in 1992, he published his autobiography, The Course of My Life, in 1998.

A worthy Merchant is the Heir of Adventure, whose hopes hang much upon the Winds.
He is a discoverer of countries and a finder-out of commodities, resolute in his attempts and royal in his Expenses.
He is the life of traffic and the Maintenance of trade, the Sailors' Master and the Soldiers' friend.
He is Neat in apparel, Modest in demeanour, dainty in diet, and Civil in his Carriage.
In sum, he is the pillar of a City, the Enricher of a Country, the furnisher of a Court, and the Worthy Servant of a King.
From _The Heir Of Adventure_ by Nicholas Breton (1545-1626)

Main photograph: 4th September 1998, Salisbury
Inset photograph: Aged 3

RICHARD ATTENBOROUGH

Lord Attenborough of Richmond upon Thames CBE
Born 1923, Cambridge

Veteran film-maker and actor, Richard Attenborough has produced and directed a string of epic movies, and starred in numerous films and stage shows, in a distinguished 60-year career.

He won a scholarship to the Royal Academy of Dramatic Art (RADA) and made his screen debut whilst still a student, in the 1942 film *In Which We Serve*. After serving in the Royal Air Force during World War Two, he won critical acclaim for his portrayal of the young thug, Pinkie, in *Brighton Rock* (1947) and went on to appear in numerous hit stage shows, such as *The Mousetrap* (1952-54), and movies such as *Private's Progress* (1956). In 1958 he became a producer, setting up two independent companies with Bryan Forbes, which spawned socially conscious films including *The Angry Silence* (1959) and the acclaimed *Seance on a Wet Afternoon* (1963).

Attenborough made his directorial debut in 1969 with the satirical musical *Oh! What A Lovely War*, which won 16 international awards including the Hollywood Golden Globe. In 1971 he led the consortium which won the franchise to establish Capital Radio, London's first independent popular music radio station, and was a leading figure in the creation of Channel Four Television, serving as Chairman from 1980-92. Knighted in 1976, he was Chairman of the British Film Institute (1981-92) and was appointed President of the British Screen Advisory Council in 1987. In 1982 he fulfilled a life-long ambition to produce and direct an epic biopic of Mahatma Gandhi. *Gandhi* won eight Oscars, including Best Picture and Best Director, and five BAFTA awards.

Attenborough went on to direct several box-office hits including *Cry Freedom* (1987), *Chaplin* (1992), *Shadowlands* (1993) and *In Love and War* (1996). After a lengthy absence from performing, he appeared in Steven Spielberg's *Jurassic Park* (1993) and its sequel *Lost World*, and played Sir William Cecil in the 1998 historical drama, *Elizabeth*. A vigorous promoter of the British film industry, he has won numerous awards, including the Evening Standard Film Award for 40 years service to British cinema in 1983. He was appointed to the Légion d'Honneur in 1988 and made a Life Peer in 1993.

The whole atmosphere and ambience of my house as I was growing up was of social awareness and social concern. It became part of my very being – like breathing. That anyone isn't concerned with these types of issues or doesn't want to do something about them, seems very odd to me. By making movies, I can express the feelings which I've had since I was a kid.

HAROLD PINTER

Harold Pinter CBE
Born 1930, Hackney, East London

Writer, actor and director, Harold Pinter has produced some of the most powerful and influential work of the post-war period. An internationally renowned playwright with a distinctly original voice, he has developed a stark, economic writing style characterised by halting dialogue, brilliantly reflective of the banalities and evasions of everyday speech.

Raised in the East End, the only son of a Jewish tailor, Pinter's childhood and adolescence, marked by evacuations during the war and anti-Semitic attacks by local fascists, engendered a sense of displacement, insecurity, isolation and suppressed violence that were to become inherent in his later work. Educated at Hackney Downs and, briefly, at drama school, Pinter was a conscientious objector to military service in 1948 and worked as an actor in repertory theatre throughout the 1950s. Inspired by Kafka and Beckett, he wrote poems, prose and plays in his spare time, and in 1957 produced his first full-length play, *The Birthday Party*. Staged in 1958, it was panned by critics in London and ran for only eight performances. His next full-length play, *The Caretaker* (1960), met with critical and commercial success, winning the *Evening Standard* award for Best Play, and confirming his position as a major figure in British theatre.

Further playwriting success followed with *The Homecoming* (1964), the one-acts *Landscape* and *Silence* (1969), *No Man's Land* (1975), *Betrayal* (1978), *A Kind of Alaska* (1982), *One for the Road* (1983), *Mountain Language* (1988) and *Party Time* (1991), the last three reflecting Pinter's concerns about political oppression and the abuse of human rights. A director of his own, and other people's, work for the stage, such as Joyce's *Exiles*, Mamet's *Oleanna* and several Simon Gray plays, Pinter has also written drama for television and radio, and screenplays for films such as *The Servant* (1963), *The French Lieutenant's Woman* (1981) and *The Comfort of Strangers* (1989).

In the mid-90s Pinter published the plays *Moonlight* and *Ashes to Ashes*. He played Harry in *The Collection*, part of the Pinter Festival at the Gate Theatre, Dublin in 1997 and at the Donmar Warehouse, London in 1998, and starred as Sir Thomas Bertram in the Miramax feature film of Jane Austen's *Mansfield Park* in 1999.

The lights glow.
What will happen next?
Poem, 1981, by Pinter

CHAD VARAH

Reverend Dr. Chad Varah CBE
Born 1911, Barton-on-Humber, Lincolnshire

Chad Varah is the founder of The Samaritans, the world-renowned organisation established in 1953 'to befriend the suicidal and despairing'.

The first of nine children born to the vicar of Barton-on-Humber, and named after a seventh-century saint, Varah was educated at Keble College, Oxford and Lincoln Theologian College. As a priest in South London, his first ministerial task had been to oversee the burial of a 13 year-old girl who had committed suicide, convinced that the blood from her menstruation was a sign of venereal disease, an incident which rapidly alerted him to the isolation and confusion that many people in his parish seemed to experience, even in the midst of traditional family units.

Commissioned to write an article on sex for the *Picture Post* magazine in 1952, Varah received a massive response from troubled readers which, combined with statistical evidence recording three suicides a day, convinced him of the need for confidential advice and support to be made available to the public. He set himself up as a counsellor in the crypt of St. Stephen's Church, Walbrook, in London, where he remains rector. Overwhelmed by people in need, Varah began to train a carefully selected band of helpers, pioneering 'listening therapy', a non-judgmental form of counselling, and presided over the sustained expansion of what became, by February 1954, The Samaritans.

Its success in providing immediate emotional support for people in crisis was such that in 1974, Varah established Befrienders International, an organisation based on the same principles, currently operating in 40 countries worldwide. In the UK, The Samaritans has become an instantly accessible, confidential safe-haven for all, comprising more than 200 branches manned by 20,000 volunteers. Formerly President of the London Branch, Varah officially retired on his 80th birthday but remains closely involved in the organisation. A prolific writer and broadcaster over the last 50 years, he is revered for his insightful intelligence, wit and generosity of spirit.

I knew for certain that neither religion nor even psychiatry was what the majority of suicidal people needed, but the 'listening therapy' we called befriending...
Befriending is beautifully aimless. It does not seek to change, reform or improve people. Those exposed to it often make changes in themselves, but that is because they want to, not because we are dissatisfied with them as they are. They have a right to be themselves.

Main photograph: 19th June 1997, St. Stephen's Church, Walbrook, London
Inset photograph: Aged 2

TWIGGY

Twiggy Lawson
Born Leslie Hornby, 1949, London

The world's first supermodel, a skinny, androgynous teenager with Bambi eyelashes and a radical haircut. Twiggy is the woman who revolutionised the shape of a generation and is synonymous with the sartorial revolution that rocked London in the 1960s.

Educated in North London, Twiggy planned to pursue her love of fashion and become a designer, but while still at school, she was persuaded by a friend to try modelling. The fashion editor of *The Women's Mirror* offered her a contract to do beauty and head shots on condition that she 'do something with her hair', and she was dispatched to Leonard's, the exclusive London hairdressers, who transformed it into a boyish, blonde bob. She was photographed by Barry Latigan, whose portraits, displayed in Leonard's salon, caught the eye of a fashion journalist with the *Daily Express*. On 23rd February 1966 a centre-page spread of the wide-eyed waif proclaimed Twiggy 'The Face of '66', and her short, but hugely successful, modelling career was launched.

She became the first international supermodel, travelling the globe and dominating the covers of all the major fashion magazines. Working with top photographers such as Richard Avedon and John Swannell, Twiggy was the most famous model in the world by the end of 1967, with a range of dresses, cosmetics and a doll to her name. In the 70s and 80s she swiftly established her credentials as an actress and musical performer, making her film debut in Ken Russell's *The Boy Friend* in 1971, for which she won critical acclaim and two Golden Globe Awards. Further film appearances included *The Blues Brothers* (1981) and *Madame Sousatzka* (1989), and she recorded a variety of albums and television shows before making her Broadway debut in the Tony award-winning Gershwin musical, *My One And Only*, in 1983.

Twiggy played Elvira in the stage show of Noel Coward's *Blithe Spirit*, hosted her own chat show for British TV and published her autobiography, *Twiggy in Black and White*, in 1997. She returned to Broadway in June 1999, playing Gertie in *If Love Were All*, a musical biography of Noel Coward and Gertrude Lawrence, directed by Leigh Lawson.

At school they'd laugh about what I looked like. I was known as Olive Oyl, because of my stick legs and Mod uniform of Hush Puppies and plastic mac flapping around my ankles. It was so hurtful. But thinking about it in retrospect, it was things like that which helped me cope with all the adulation that followed. Because I never really believed a word of it, and thought they were all mad.

JACK JONES

Jack Jones CH, MBE
Born 1913, Liverpool

Jack Jones has been one of the most influential figures in the British trade union movement this century. Nick-named 'Emperor Jones', he has devoted his life to improving conditions for working people and has introduced significant changes to facilitate industrial democracy.

The son of a Liverpool docker, Jones left school at 14 to work as an engineering apprentice before following his father to the docks, where he witnessed the hardship and poverty of the 1930s Depression. He continued his studies at night school and at the age of just 15, became local ward secretary to the Labour Party. At 17 he was a delegate to the Labour Trades Council and at 23, he was elected a city councillor. He fought in the Spanish Civil War and was wounded at the battle of Ebro in 1938. During World War Two he became a full-time official at the Transport and General Workers' Union (TGWU) in Coventry and helped keep the munitions industry working throughout the bombing of the city.

After the war, Jones organised the work force of the car industry in the Midlands for a period, and served as the Regional Secretary of the TGWU. He fought throughout the 50s and 60s to provide greater representation of workers and campaigned for the development of the shop steward system, encouraging union officials to work with, and formally recognise, shop stewards. In 1968 he was elected General Secretary of the TGWU and during his nine years at the helm, built the organisation into the largest and most powerful union in the world. A leading advocate for the creation of an independent organisation to which workers and their employees could take their disputes, he was one of the first 12 members appointed to the Advisory, Conciliation and Arbitration Service (ACAS) in 1974, which replaced the government-controlled Conciliation and Advisory Service. He held prominent positions in the Trades Union Congress, actively encouraged the appointment of women as union officials and was a leading spokesman on international and economic issues.

Jones retired in 1978, but has continued to fly the flag for justice, serving as Vice-President of the Anti-Apartheid Movement since 1976 and Age Concern since 1978. He has been President of the Retired Members Association since 1979 and Chairman of the National Pensioners' Convention since 1992.

The flame of freedom, the flame of understanding for a better society is still there. It flickers, but it's still there, it's still burning and it'll go into flame again.

Main photograph: 5th May 1998, Transport House, Victoria, London
Inset photograph: In 1936, Liverpool

CLIFF RICHARD

Sir Cliff Richard OBE
Born Harry Webb, 1940, Lucknow, India

Britain's most enduringly popular recording artist, Cliff Richard holds the prestigious position of being the only singer to have scored a UK Number One single in five successive decades from the 1950s to the 1990s. In a career spanning virtually the entire history of British rock music, the born-again Christian singer and actor has combined chart-topping success with a lasting commitment to charity work.

Richard arrived in Britain in 1948 and began work as an office clerk, forming an up-tempo rock'n'roll group, The Drifters, with Terry Smart and Ian Samwell, in 1957, aged 17. Signed by EMI's Columbia label in 1958, their debut single, *Move It*, reached number two in the charts. A re-organised line-up incorporated guitarists Hank Marvin and Bruce Welch, soon to become The Shadows, and introduced a softer-beat ballad style, which resulted in two Number One hits, the now legendary *Living Doll*, and *Travellin' Light*.

During the next four years Richard had 17 Top Ten hits in Britain, including *Please Don't Tease* and *I Love You*, and appeared in several youth-orientated movies, most notably *The Young Ones* in 1962, which catapulted him to international stardom. The title track was a Number One hit, and the follow-up film, the now classic *Summer Holiday* (1963), whose title track also hit the top spot, confirmed his status as the British Elvis Presley. Despite the advent of Beatlemania, Richard's handsome, clean-living image had engendered widespread appeal, and he enjoyed 12 Top Ten hits in the mid-60s, culminating in *Congratulations* in 1968, which topped the UK and European charts.

In 1969 Richard left The Shadows to embark on a solo career, trading on the success of his clear, precise singing voice, and a partnership with writer/producer Alan Tarney resulted in a more contemporary musical style in the 70s, with hits such as *Devil Woman* (1976) and *We Don't Talk Anymore* (1979). Highlights of the 80s included duets with Olivia Newton John and Van Morrisson, a Christmas Number One with *Mistletoe and Wine* and a million-selling album, *Private Collection* (1988). A Christmas Number One in 1990, *Saviour's Day*, launched the decade which saw his 35th Top Five single, his knighthood in 1995 and his lead in the musical *Heathcliffe* in 1996, which broke box office records for first week-ticket sales.

A multi-award winner, Richard celebrated his 40th anniversary in the music industry in 1998 with a hit album, *Real As I Wanna Be*, and a sell-out concert at London's Royal Albert Hall.

Rock'n'roll and God work well together in the hands of someone who loves them both.

Main photograph: 25th September 1998, Claygate, Surrey
Inset photograph: Aged 4

STEVE REDGRAVE

Steven Redgrave CBE
Born 1962, Amersham, Buckinghamshire

The world's most outstanding rower of all time, Steve Redgrave has achieved an unprecedented performance in world rowing as the winner of four consecutive Olympic gold medals, a record matched by only five other sportsmen in 100 years of Olympic history.

Educated at Great Marlow school, Redgrave joined the Marlow Rowing Club in 1976, aged 14, and began competing in junior events before achieving his first success as runner-up in the World Junior double sculls in 1980. The following year he made his World Senior debut in the quad sculls event before claiming his first victory in the Henley Royal Regatta Diamond Sculls in 1983.

Selected for the British Olympic Team in 1984, aged 22, he won his first gold medal in the coxed fours event at the 1984 Los Angeles Olympics, and produced spectacular performances in 1986 with a record three golds at the Commonwealth Games in Edinburgh for the single scull, coxless pairs and coxed fours events. Teaming up with Andy Holmes, he seized his next Olympic gold for the coxless pairs event (2000m) in Seoul in 1988 and, a year later, began what was to become a formidable partnership with British team member Matthew Pinsent. The seemingly unbeatable duo, famous for their powerful finishes, won gold in the coxless pairs events at the 1992 Barcelona Olympics and the 1996 Atlanta games.

In addition to his Olympic successes, Redgrave has dominated the World Championships for the past 12 years, winning eight gold medals. In 1986 and 1987 he was teamed with Holmes in the coxless pairs event, and then with Pinsent in 1991, 1993, 1994 and 1995. After the Atlanta Olympics Redgrave officially retired, but within a month had returned to the water, and in 1997 he and Pinsent joined Tim Foster and James Cracknell to form a coxless four and won the 1997 and 1998 World Championships.

Redgrave was awarded the MBE in 1987 and the CBE in 1997, and is heralded as the greatest Olympian Britain has ever produced.

If I ever row again, you have my permission to shoot me!
Post-retirement, pre-comeback, Atlanta, 1996.

MICHAEL CARVER

Field Marshal Lord Carver, GCB, CBE, DSO, MC
Born 1915, Surrey

Former Chief of Defence Staff, military tactician and the Army's youngest brigade commander during the Second World War, Michael Carver is one of Britain's most distinguished soldiers. He has served in Kenya, Cyprus, Singapore and Northern Ireland and been a key figure in major defence policy decisions throughout his 43-year career.

Educated at Winchester College, Carver considered joining the priesthood before opting for the army. He trained at Sandhurst and was commissioned as a Second Lieutenant in the Royal Tank Corps in 1935. Peacetime soldiering in Egypt was followed by service in the 7th Armoured Division in North Africa at the start of World War Two. He took part in the Battle of El Alamein and the Normandy landings, and at just 29, commanded the 4th Independent Armoured Brigade in North West Europe. He was awarded the Military Cross in 1942 and appointed Member of the Distinguished Service Order in 1943.

After the war, Carver went on to hold a number of high ranking military posts, including Director of Army Staff Duties at the Ministry of Defence (1964-66), where he was involved in the restructuring of the armed forces, and was knighted in 1966. He was Commander-in-Chief Far East (1967-69), during which time he oversaw Britain's withdrawal from South East Asia, and Chief of General Staff (1971-73) during some of the worst violence in Northern Ireland. In 1973 he was appointed Chief of Defence Staff, where he made a significant contribution to formulating Britain's defence policy within NATO, and was made a Field Marshal.

Following his retirement from the Army, he became Resident Commissioner (Designate) in Rhodesia (1977-78) during the negotiations for the transition to majority rule, and was made a Life Peer. He was later influential in the formulation of Britain's nuclear and conventional weapons policy, and has written widely on military issues.

As one who, gazing at a vista
Of beauty, sees the clouds close in,
And turns his back on sorrow, hearing
The thunderclouds begin.

So we, whose life was all before us,
Our hearts with sunlight filled,
Left in the hills our books and flowers,
Descended, and were killed.

Write on the stones no words of sadness -
Only the gladness due,
That we, who asked the most of living,
Knew how to give it too.

Pollitici Meliora (Having Promised Better Things) 1943
by Frank Thompson, poet and soldier, executed in Bulgaria
while on SOE mission in 1944

Main photograph: 28th April 1998
     Inset photograph: Aged 8

CLIVE SINCLAIR

Sir Clive Sinclair
Born 1940, London

Clive Sinclair is the inventor who brought the pocket calculator, portable TV, digital watch and first affordable, mass-marketed computer into British homes. An electronics entrepreneur, he is famous for his miniaturisation of modern consumer goods and his commitment to developing low-cost, environmentally friendly modes of transport.

The son of a mechanical engineer, Sinclair thrilled his classmates as a child with home-made rockets and stink-bombs, and at the age of 11, devised the binary system of mathematical notation before discovering that it had already been invented. In 1962 he founded Sinclair Radionics and produced a variety of miniature electronic goods, such as a matchbox-sized radio and amplifier kits sold through mail-order.

He became a household name in 1967 with the launch of the world's first pocket calculator, an instant success which won numerous design awards. He went on to dominate the calculator market with the Sinclair Cambridge range and introduced a low-cost, digital multimeter in 1975. The same year he employed the new circuit technology to produce the best-selling digital watch, the Black Watch, and launched Microvision, a pocket television, two years later.

He founded Sinclair Research in 1979 and won international acclaim for his Sinclair ZX80, the first personal computer to sell for under £100.00. In 1981 he produced an upgraded model, the ZX81, which sold over a million units and won the Design Council Award.

It was the colour ZX Spectrum, however, a disposable plastic computer with sponge-like keyboard, which became the market leader for a decade. Launched in 1982, it spawned a lively computer games scene in Britain and earned its creator a knighthood in 1983.

Sinclair founded Sinclair Vehicles in 1984 to develop electric modes of transport and gained admiration and derision in equal measure for his eccentric C5 electric tricycle in 1985. Pursuing the idea of low-cost, pollution-free transport, he launched Zike, an electric bicycle, in 1992 and ZETA, a conversion kit which adds electrical assistance to ordinary push-bikes, in 1994.

In 1997 he produced the Sinclair X1 Button FM Radio, the world's smallest radio weighing just half an ounce, and launched the Z1 Micro AM Radio in 1999.

In each case, I wanted to find a need, to come up with something that people would then need. Take the pocket calculator: no-one was going around saying that they needed one, but once they'd got it, they needed it. It's about finding something that will be useful to people, and changing the world in a small way.

LEW GRADE

Lord Grade of Elstree
Born Louis Winogradsky, 1906, Tokmak, Russia

Legendary film and television impresario Lew Grade was one of the most colourful and influential figures of British popular entertainment. A showbusiness entrepreneur and television tycoon, he famously turned wheeler-dealing into a creative art and had an uncanny instinct for knowing what his audience wanted.

Arriving in Britain in 1912, he began work in the family embroidery business, aged 14. A keen dancer, he won the 1926 World Championship Charleston Competition and toured Europe as a professional performer, newly named 'Lew Grade'. In 1933 he set up a theatrical agency with his brother which became the largest in Europe, and helped launch the careers of stars such as Norman Wisdom and Morecambe and Wise. After serving briefly with the Royal Signal Corps during World War Two, Grade began developing a two-way traffic in international talent and brought American stars such as Frank Sinatra, Bob Hope and Sammy Davis Jnr. to Britain.

He became a pioneer of independent television and launched Associated Television in 1954, which became Associated Communications Corporation (ACC), and as its Chairman of 28 years, oversaw some of the most successful series of the times, such as *Robin Hood*, *The Saint*, *Thunderbirds*, *The Persuaders*, *Joe 90*, *The Prisoner*, *The Muppet Show* and the soap, *Crossroads*, which ran for 24 years. Grade recognised the potential of selling British-made shows to the United States and by the late 60s, his company was selling more programmes overseas than all the other ITV companies and the BBC put together. In 1969 he was knighted for services to export.

ACC developed into an international empire spanning music, theatre, cinema and merchandising, and produced feature films such as *The Eagle Has Landed* (1976), *The Boys From Brazil* (1978), two *Pink Panther* comedies and *The Muppet Movie* (1979), as well as drama specials for the American television networks such as the epic, critically acclaimed *Jesus of Nazareth*. A lover of big-budget extravaganzas, Grade's costly 1980 film *Raise the Titanic* was poorly received, prompting his rueful observation that 'It would have been cheaper to lower the Atlantic', but he bounced back with the award-winning, box-office hits *On Golden Pond* (1981) and *Sophie's Choice* (1982).

Grade was made a Life Peer in 1976 and among many honours, was the recipient of the Knight Commander of The Order of St. Silvestre, with an additional Order of a Star, by Pope John Paul II in 1979. He was Chairman of Embassy Communications International from 1982 until 1985, when he set up The Grade Company, and produced several films for TV based on the novels of Barbara Cartland and his last feature film, *Something To Believe In* (1998). He died on December 13th 1998.

There are only three things that count in life. One is your family. Two is your health and three is relationships. The rest doesn't matter.

BARBARA CASTLE

The Rt. Hon. Baroness Castle of Blackburn
Born Barbara Betts, 1911, Chesterfield, Derbyshire

Hailed as 'The First Lady of Socialism', Barbara Castle has led an energetic and colourful political career, spanning more than half a century. A staunch defender of the Welfare State, she famously battled for equal pay in the 1970s and has been a vociferous campaigner for the maintenance of state insurance.

Educated at Oxford University, Castle began her career in local government in 1937 and was one of the youngest members elected to the St. Pancras Borough Council. She was an air-raid warden during the London blitzes and became the voice of the armed forces on the Daily Mirror. In 1945 she entered parliament as an MP for Blackburn. A member of the National Executive of the Labour Party from 1950-79, she served as party chairman from 1958-59. A committed 'Bevanite', she rapidly made her name as an outspoken defender of left-wing causes.

In 1964 Castle was appointed the first ever Minister of Overseas Development in Harold Wilson's government, before being promoted to Minister of Transport (1965-68), during which time she introduced the 70 mph speed limit, the 'breathalyser' test for drunken drivers and an integrated transport policy. In 1968 she was again promoted by Wilson, this time to First Secretary of State for Employment and Productivity. In this capacity she piloted the Equal Pay Act through parliament in 1970 and caused controversy with her policies on trade union reform outlined in her White Paper, In Place of Strife.

In 1974, after four years in opposition, Labour was returned to power and Castle was appointed Secretary of State for Social Security, where she carried through far-reaching plans to modernise the Beveridge Report On Social Insurance And Allied Services, by strengthening the system of state insurance and introducing child benefit. When James Callaghan replaced Harold Wilson as Prime Minister in 1976 she was removed to the back benches and left Westminster three years later to become the leader of the British Labour Group in the European Parliament (1979-85).

Castle has continued to campaign for her beliefs both through the publication of her frank Cabinet diaries, *The Castle Diaries 1964-1976*, and her autobiography, *Fighting All The Way* (1993). Created a Life Peer in 1990, she went on to champion the rights of pensioners and in 1996, co-wrote the pamphlet, *We Can Afford The Welfare State*.

On we march then, we the workers, and the rumour that ye hear
Is the blended sound of battle and deliv'rance drawing near:
For the hope of every creature is the banner that we bear,
And the world is marching on.
From *The March of the Workers*, by William Morris (1834-1896)

Main photograph: 21st April 1999, High Wycombe.
Inset photograph: Aged 14

JOHN MILLS

Sir John Mills CBE
Born 1908, North Elmham, Suffolk

Oscar-winning actor John Mills is one of Britain's most popular and prolific performers. Best known for his portrayal of the quintessential Englishman in the patriotic films of the 1940s, he has appeared in 90 films and numerous stage and television shows in a career spanning almost seventy years.

Born into a theatrical family, Mills made his stage debut as a chorus boy in *The Five O'Clock Revue* in London in 1927. He progressed to more prestigious theatre roles in *Cavalcade* (1931) and *Words and Music* (1932) before making his screen debut as a sailor in *The Midshipmaid* (1932). Following military service, he rose to prominence playing a variety of heroic servicemen in films such as *In Which We Serve* (1942) and the *The Way to the Stars* (1945).

His highly acclaimed portrayal of the adult Pip in David Lean's production of *Great Expectations* (1946) secured him a contract with the Rank Organisation, and he went on to win numerous awards for his portrayal of the British hero *Scott of the Antarctic* (1948) and was hailed as the definitive Mr Polly in H.G Wells's *The History of Mr. Polly* (1949). A top box office star throughout the 1940s and 50s, he epitomised the classic British virtues of integrity and stoicism in memorable films such as *The Colditz Story* (1955) and *Ice Cold In Alex* (1958).

Awarded the CBE in 1960, Mills made his directoral debut with the film *Sky West and Crooked* (1965) before performing one of his most celebrated roles, Field Marshal Sir Douglas Haig in Richard Attenborough's 1969 film version of *Oh! What A Lovely War*. In 1970 he won an Oscar for Best Supporting Actor for his role as the village idiot in *Ryan's Daughter* (1970), and made cameo appearances in films such as *Young Winston* (1972) and *Gandhi* (1982). Knighted in 1979, he has starred in numerous television series, such as the ITV science fiction drama *Quatermass*, and played Old Chuffey in the 1995 BBC adaptation of Dickens's *Martin Chuzzlewit*.

The holder of 18 national and international awards as Best Actor, Mills returned to the big screen in 1996, aged 88, for a highly acclaimed performance as Old Norway in Kenneth Branagh's *Hamlet*.

Do not despair
For Johnny-head-in-air,
He sleeps as sound
As Johnny underground.

Fetch out no shroud
For Johnny-in-the-cloud;
And keep your tears
For him in after years.

Better by far
For Johnny the bright star
To keep your head,
And see his children fed.
Johnny-Head-in-Air, by John Pudney, 1973

Main photograph: 11th August 1998, Denham, Buckinghamshire
Inset photograph: Aged 8, as Puck in the school production of Shakespeare's *A Midsummer Night's Dream*

TONY WARREN

Tony Warren
Born 1936. Manchester

Tony Warren is the creator of the world's longest-running and most successful television soap opera, *Coronation Street*, a fictional backstreet of terraced houses located in the industrial heart of northern England. The fortunes of its inhabitants, and the gritty depiction of their working lives, have regularly gripped over 18 million viewers for 39 years, confirming the *Street*'s status as a venerable national institution.

The son of a fruit importer, Warren was educated at Eccles Grammar School, where he gained a reputation for truancy, preferring to spend his time absorbing theatrical biographies in Manchester's Central Library. Enthralled by showbusiness, he embarked on a career as an actor, performing in BBC radio drama broadcasts, aged just 12, and progressing to roles in television, film and theatre.

In 1958 he discovered that Granada Television were looking for new writers, and submitted a script for their detective show, *Shadow Squad*, with an enigmatic note attached, saying 'If you want to know how this ends, telephone Pendleton 2437'. He was hired on an exclusive one-year contract and wrote a variety of scripts, including episodes of *Biggles*. Desperate to write drama reflective of the social climate of the north, he presented his bosses with the synopsis of a new show called *Florizel Street*. A mixture of comedy and drama, dominated by powerful, passionate female characters drawn with acute perception from his own matriarchal background, it was an instant hit. On the recommendation of a Granada tea lady, who complained that the street name sounded like a brand of disinfectant, the series became *Coronation Street*, and episode one was aired on 9th December 1960.

Warren wrote the first 14 programmes and many subsequent episodes during the following decades, as well as penning the 60s television trilogy *The War of Darkie Pilbeam* and the 1964 film *Ferry 'Cross The Mersey*. He returned to prominence in 1991 with a best-selling novel, *The Lights of Manchester*, and quickly established himself as a serious fiction writer, publishing *Foot of the Rainbow* in 1993, *Behind Closed Doors* in 1995 and *Full Steam Ahead* in 1998.

You closed your eyes and you could see the pot flights of ducks, and the antimacassars, and the chenille tablecloths, and the newspapers stuffed under the cushion of the easy chair. You sniffed and you could smell the burning sausages, and the cheap hairspray and the tang of bitter beer.
Harry Kershaw, Granada Television producer, on reading the first *Coronation Street* script submitted by Warren, 1960

Main photograph: 2nd November 1998, Coronation Street, Manchester
Inset photograph: Aged 15

ANDREW LLOYD WEBBER

Lord Lloyd Webber of Sydmonton in the County of Hampshire
Born 1948, London

Andrew Lloyd Webber is the foremost theatrical composer of our time. Credited with reinventing the modern musical, his innovative and memorable scores for a series of spectacular productions have been performed in 20 countries worldwide during the past 30 years.

The son of a distinguished organist and choirmaster, Lloyd Webber had written his first composition by the age of seven. A student at the Royal College of Music, he met budding lyricist Tim Rice in 1965 and the result of their first collaboration was the stunning 'pop oratorio' *Joseph and the Amazing Technicolor Dreamcoat*. An exuberant rock'n'roll reworking of the biblical story, it premiered at Colet Court School, Hammersmith in 1968, opened in the West End in 1973 and on Broadway in 1982, and was an instant hit. They followed it with *Jesus Christ Superstar*, which opened to ecstatic reviews in London in 1972, ran for eight years and generated record-breaking album sales, and then premiered *Evita* in 1976. A huge success, it won a gold disc for the song *Don't Cry For Me Argentina*, seized seven Tony awards in America, including Best Score and Best Musical, and formed the basis of Alan Parker's movie *Evita* in 1996, for which they won the Golden Globe and an Oscar for Best Original Song.

In 1978 Lloyd Webber formed *The Really Useful Company*, to produce his own, and other people's, works. T.S.Eliot's collection of poems in the *Old Possum's Book of Practical Cats* was the inspiration for his next smash-hit, *CATS*, which opened at the New London Theatre in 1981, co-produced by Cameron Mackintosh, and is the longest-running musical in the history of the West End and Broadway. *Song and Dance* opened in 1982 and was followed by *Starlight Express* in 1984, which became the second longest-running musical in London. Lloyd Webber's 1986 production *The Phantom of the Opera* won the Laurence Olivier and Evening Standard awards for Best Musical, garnered seven Tony awards and by 1999 had been viewed by an estimated 52 million people worldwide. Further successes followed with *Aspects of Love* in 1989, *Sunset Boulevard* in 1993 and *Whistle Down the Wind* in 1998.

Lloyd Webber was knighted in 1992 and appointed a Life Peer in 1994.

I was a shmuck at school because I liked *The Sound of Music*. Musical theatre is the only thing that has ever made me tick. Whatever happens, success or failure, I'll still be there.

Main photograph: 22nd April 1999, London
Inset photograph: Aged 8, in Trafalgar Square

ROY CALNE

Sir Roy Calne MS, FRCS, FRS
Born 1930, Richmond, Surrey

Eminent surgeon Roy Calne is the foremost pioneer of liver transplantation in Britain. His research into overcoming donor organ rejection has resulted in widespread advancement in donor organ transplantation programmes around the world.

Graduating from Guy's Hospital Medical School in London in 1952, Calne undertook his national service as a medical officer in the Far East before returning to London in 1958 to train at the Royal Free Hospital. He began researching kidney transplantation in 1959 and focused on the problem of organ rejection, which was proving the greatest obstruction to successful donor organ surgery. Experimentation resulted in his first triumph in 1960, the discovery that the new anti-cancer drug, Azathioprine, prevented the rejection of patients' grafts and dramatically improved the success rate of future kidney transplant operations.

Appointed Professor of Surgery at the University of Cambridge in 1965, Calne set up the kidney transplant programme at Addenbrooke's Hospital where 1,600 successful operations have since been performed. He embarked on extensive research into liver transplantation and forged major advances in scientific knowledge and surgical expertise, which established him as the world's leading expert in the field. In 1968 he began the first European Liver Transplant Programme, and in 1978 he achieved his second major breakthrough with the development and clinical use of the potent new immuno-suppressant drug, Cyclosporin, which also diminished the risk of graft rejection. In 1979 he performed the first pancreas transplant in the UK, and in December 1986 he and fellow surgeon John Wallwork led a 15-strong team who performed the first ever heart-lung-liver transplant at Papworth Hospital, in Cambridge. Six years later, he performed the first intestinal transplant in the UK.

Knighted in 1986, Calne is a Fellow of the Royal Society and has held numerous academic and medical posts, including that of President of the International Transplant Society (1992-94). He retired in 1998 but continues to campaign for greater government involvement in donor organ programmes.

'What a piece of work is a man! how noble in reason! how infinite in faculty!
in form and moving how express and admirable! in action, how like an angel!
in apprehension, how like a god!'
Hamlet, Act II, Scene II, *Hamlet*, by William Shakespeare

Main photograph: 17 December 1998, Cambridge
Inset photograph: Aged 2

DAVID BOWIE

David Bowie
Born David Robert Jones, 1947, Brixton, London

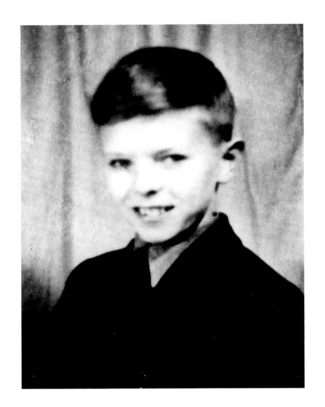

Musician, performer and songwriter, David Bowie has remained at the pinnacle of the performing arts scene for three decades. Renowned for continually re-inventing his image and his art, he has pioneered fashion, moulded the zeitgeist, manipulated the media and marketed himself as one of the most enduring, enigmatic and influential artists of all time.

Bowie began playing the saxophone in his teens and joined bands such as the King Bees, the Manish Boys and the Lower Third. After a slow start, his single *Space Oddity* reached Number 5 in the UK Charts in 1969, and he followed it with his first album, *The Man Who Sold The World* (1970), which heralded the emergence of glam rock. After *Hunky Dory* (1971) he adopted the persona of his rock'n'roll creation Ziggy, with the release of *The Rise And Fall Of Ziggy Stardust And The Spiders From Mars* (1972). The album was an instant hit and its accompanying tour, featuring spectacular Japanese costumes and snarling guitars, was more rock theatre than traditional concert. In 1973 *Aladdin Sane* topped the UK album charts, following the retirement of *Ziggy Stardust*, and in 1975 Bowie metamorphosed into the White Soul Boy with Young Americans, achieving his first US Number One with the single Fame.

Bowie made his feature film debut as an alien in Nicholas Roeg's *The Man Who Fell To Earth* in 1976 before engineering his next incarnation as the Thin White Duke for the funk-influenced album, *Station To Station*. In 1977 he collaborated with Brian Eno and Tony Visconti in Berlin to produce the predominantly instrumental, ambient albums *Low* and *Heroes*, and appeared in the film *Just a Gigolo*. Touring between recordings, he received rave reviews for his Broadway debut in the title role of *The Elephant Man* in 1980 and released the *Scary Monsters* album. In 1982 he played the male lead in the film *The Hunger* and appeared in *Merry Christmas, Mr. Lawrence*. In 1983 he released *Let's Dance*, whose title track gave him his third UK Number One and which featured the Motown-styled Modern Love and the darkly romantic *China Girl*. In 1988, he formed the band Tin Machine, a modern alternative act with a stripped-down guitar sound.

Bowie returned to solo projects in 1993 with *Black Tie White Noise*, which entered the UK album charts at Number One, and produced one of rock's first CD-ROMs, *Jump*. Ever operating on the cutting edge, he broke new ground with the Internet-only release of the drum'n'bass single, *Telling Lies*, and in 1998 launched BowieNet, the first individualised Internet service provider, rated 'the coolest site on the planet' by PC Magazine.

We have created a child who will be so exposed to the media that he will be lost to his parents by the time he is twelve.
1972

DENYS LASDUN

Sir Denys Lasdun CH, CBE, RA, RIBA
Born 1914, London

Celebrated as the founding father of modern British architecture, Denys Lasdun has left an indelible mark on the London skyline. Through all of his works, from housing projects to the acclaimed Royal National Theatre, he has set out to re-define architecture and promote the philosophy that architecture be regarded as 'urban landscape', a social art designed for the people.

Educated at Rugby and the Architecture Association in London, Lasdun went into practice with the pioneering modernist architect Wells Coates from 1935-37, before joining the Tecton partnership of Lubetkin, Skinner and Drake in 1938. After distinguished service in The Royal Engineers in World War Two, for which he was awarded the MBE, he became a partner of Tecton, designing housing projects such as the flats on the Paddington Estate (1948). In 1949 he teamed up with architect Lindsey Drake and designed flats in St James's Place, London (1958) and Fitzwilliam College in Cambridge (1959).

A year later he set up his own London practice and established himself as one of Britain's leading architects with his brutalist design for the Royal College of Physicians in Regent's Park, London (1961-64), and the University of East Anglia, Norwich (1962-68). His best known and most controversial building, however, is the National Theatre, an imposing monument of concrete terraces astride London's South Bank, which was completed in 1976. A bold, innovative but highly criticised design, it was nevertheless heralded as a milestone of modern architecture. He followed it with the Mediterranean-style, white concrete School of Oriental and African Studies for London University (1970-73) and the acclaimed European Investment Bank in Luxembourg in 1975.

A teacher and lecturer during the 60s and 70s, Lasdun has been a Fellow of the Royal Institute of British Architects since 1945 and a member of the Council of the Architectural Association since 1974. He was knighted in 1976 and made a Companion of Honour in 1995.

Architecture, for me at any rate, only makes sense as a promoter and extender of human relations. But it has to communicate through the language of form and space if it is to be considered an art. This implies giving form: touching the spirit; bearing the imprint of sensibility, temperament and intellect; concern for the immeasurable; the capacity to make value judgements as to what is ugly, what is beautiful, organising plans that are in touch with life – a quality very quickly sensed by the man on the street.

ANITA RODDICK

Anita Roddick OBE
Born Anita Perilli, 1942, Littlehampton, East Sussex

Founder of the 'green' skin and hair care products chain, The Body Shop, Anita Roddick has spawned a cosmetics empire comprising over 1,800 outlets in 48 countries worldwide. A vociferous campaigner against cosmetics testing on animals and a promoter of recycling, she has built a business based on ethical values that have challenged the ethos of the beauty industry and increased awareness of environmentalism.

The daughter of Italian immigrants, Roddick qualified as a teacher from Newton College of Education in Bath in 1963, and after numerous teaching posts, embarked on a year-long trip around the world, taking in the Polynesian Islands and Indian Ocean Islands before returning to London in 1968. Inspired by the women in pre-industrial countries who based their beauty preparations on natural herbal remedies, she decided to set up a small business producing skin care products based on a similar approach. Substituting enthusiasm for formal business training, she opened The Body Shop in Brighton in 1976 with just 30 hand-mixed products on sale, and after high summer sales, opened a second store six months later.

Committed to developing a business that could generate social change as well as profits, and aided by her husband Gordon, Roddick's environmentally-friendly, nut-and-berry based lotions and citrus-scented potions tapped into a lucrative niche market. High profile campaigns urged customers to support issues such as human rights and the protection of indigenous people, and to eradicate poverty, avoid pollution and prevent wars. The practice of recycling, whereby customers were encouraged to bring in old bottles for refill, rapidly became an intrinsic part of the company's doctrine, and through its sourcing of ingredients from ethnic communities, The Body Shop developed a community trade programme, 'Trade Not Aid', creating sustainable trading relationships with communities in need.

Hailed as a role model for women, Roddick has won numerous honorary doctorates and business accolades, including the UK Women of Achievement Award (1988) and the UN Environmental Award (1989), and was voted the Most Admired Business Woman in the UK in 1995.

If a woman can figure out which one gets the last toffee, the four year-old or the six year-old, she can negotiate any contract in the world.

TOM KILBURN

Professor Kilburn CBE, FREng, FRS
Born 1921, Earlsheaton, West Yorkshire

Tom Kilburn is the co-creator of the world's first stored programme computer, a one-ton, 18ft long giant called the 'Baby' which leapt into life at 11.00am on June 21st 1948 and launched the computer age.

A maths graduate from Cambridge University, Kilburn worked with leading circuit designer Freddie Williams during World War Two. In 1946 he joined Williams, who had been appointed Professor of Electro-Technics at Manchester University, to continue work on developing digital storage of information. At the time, there were only two electronic computers operational in the world, ENIAC in America, built for ballistics, and Colossus, built at Bletchley Park to crack the German Engima codes, but both lacked memory and the race was on to produce the first modern computer. The two designed and built 'Baby', a small-scale experimental machine, the Mark 1 prototype, and by using a cathode-ray tube (CRT) with electrical charges stored inside it, were able to create the first random access memory (RAM). They inserted a programme, written by Kilburn on the train to work in the mornings, many times without success until one day the Baby worked out the highest factor of 31, and changed the face of technology forever.

The Baby was powered by 3,500 watts of electricity, had a memory capacity of 128 bytes and performed 700 instructions a second, in contrast to the 50 million carried out by today's computers with 32 million bytes. Its computing power was less than that of a modern calculator but it could solve mathematical problems 10,000 times faster than ever before and presented limitless possibilities. The CRT store was patented in 1946, Kilburn was awarded a PhD for his work and the government granted over a million pounds for further research. The Mark 1, built in 1951 by the UK-based company Ferranti, was the first commercial computer to be delivered.

Kilburn went on to build the first operational transistor computer in 1953 and followed it with the Atlas computer in 1962, which boasted the first real, read-only memory (ROM) and the first virtual memory, with UK institutes accessing it via telephone cables. He founded the Computer Science Department at Manchester University in 1964 and, with his colleagues, drafted a curriculum for the first degree course in computing at a UK university. He became Emeritus Professor of Computer Science and retired in 1981, after 35 years of computer research and teaching.

It worked. There was euphoria. Geoff Tootill, my assistant, and I danced up and down. Freddie and I knew we could build an extended version that would be very significant in scientific and mathematical work. But did we know what would happen in the following 50 years? No!

Main photograph: 2nd November 1998, in front of a full-size model of the 'Baby'
Inset photograph: Aged 26

ALAN AYCKBOURN

Sir Alan Ayckbourn CBE
Born 1939, London

Alan Ayckbourn is one of Britain's most prolific and successful playwrights, celebrated for his poignant observations of the English middle classes. His large body of work comprises 54 plays which range from the very light to the very dark, in addition to adaptations, revues and shorter entertainments.

Educated at Haileybury public school, Ayckbourn got his first job, aged 17, with Donald Wolfit's company, as actor and assistant stage manager on the classic production of *The Strong are Lonely* at the Edinburgh Festival in 1956. A year later, he joined The Studio Theatre Company run by Stephen Joseph, the pioneer in Britain of theatre-in-the-round, who had acquired two rooms in Scarborough's public library to present a series of plays. Encouraged by Joseph, Ayckbourn penned his first professional play in 1959, a comedy entitled *The Square Cat*, which opened in Scarborough to great acclaim.

Mr. Whatnot, written in 1963, was the first of his plays to transfer to London's West End, but it was the smash hit *Relatively Speaking*, a comedy of misunderstandings now hailed as a classic, which propelled him to celebrity, opening at the Duke of York's Theatre in London in 1967. In 1971 he became Artistic Director of Scarborough's Theatre-in-the-Round company and went on to write numerous hit plays, notably *Absurd Person Singular* (1972), *The Norman Conquests* (1973), *Just Between Ourselves* (1975), *A Chorus of Disapproval* (1984), *Woman In Mind* (1985), *Man of the Moment* (1988) and *Things We Do For Love* (1997).

An established director, Ayckbourn was invited to direct four plays at the National Theatre in the mid-80s, winning a Plays and Players Director of the Year Award for his production of Arthur Miller's *A View From the Bridge*. A writer of children's plays as well as musicals, including *By Jeeves* (1996) with Andrew Lloyd Webber, he finally realised his ambition to establish a permanent home for the Theatre-in-the-Round company in Scarborough with the opening of the Stephen Joseph Theatre in 1996. Awarded the CBE in 1987, Ayckbourn was knighted for services to theatre in 1997.

Is there anybody out there?

Main photograph: 17th January 1999, Wapping, London
Inset photograph: Aged 6

CICELY SAUNDERS

Dame Cicely Saunders OM, FRCP, FRCS
Born 1918, Barnet, Greater London

Cicely Saunders is the former nurse who pioneered the modern hospice movement in Britain and revolutionised palliative care for the dying. Her philosophy of care combined with effective and holistic pain control has led to a profound change in medical and nursing attitudes towards death and dying throughout the world.

Saunders trained as a nurse at the Nightingale School in London and read Social Sciences at Oxford University. Her early nursing experience exposed her to the inadequacy of care available for the terminally ill, and after a period working as a voluntary medical social worker at St. Luke's in Bayswater, one of the few homes for the dying, she decided to retrain as a doctor. Qualifying from St. Thomas's in 1957, she was awarded a fellowship by St. Mary's Medical School to work at St. Joseph's Hospice, where she pursued her interest in holistic pain control and studied analgesia.

Saunders began to develop her vision of a modern home for the dying, and published numerous articles calling for support from the profession. Combining her Christian beliefs with medical expertise, she promoted the principles of dying with dignity, maintaining that death is a natural part of living rather than a medical failure, and gained widespread recognition for her assertion that its quality could be greatly enhanced by sensitive nursing and effective pain control. Awarded the OBE in 1967, she oversaw the opening of St. Christopher's Hospice in the same year, fulfilling a dream she had held since 1948, when a young Jewish patient left her £500, saying that he wanted to be a window in her home. Whilst not the first British hospice, St. Christopher's rapidly became the prototype for modern research and teaching hospices throughout the world, rooted in the philosophy that carers not only strive to free patients from pain and distress, but learn 'how to be silent, how to listen, and how just to be there.'

A prolific writer and researcher, Saunders has received numerous awards for her contribution to medicine, including the Templeton Foundation Prize in 1981. She became a Dame of the British Empire in 1980 and received the Order of Merit in 1989.

You matter because you are you and you matter to the last moment of your life. We will do all we can, not only to help you die peacefully but also to live until you die.

Main photograph: 31st March 1999, London
Inset photograph: Aged 4

GEORGE WEIDENFELD

Lord Weidenfeld of Chelsea
Born 1919, Vienna, Austria

Publisher George Weidenfeld has been responsible for the publication and commissioning of some of the most influential works of English literature this century, from Vladimir Nabokov's *Lolita* to internationally acclaimed historical and political biographies. A charismatic and entrepreneurial figure, he has built Weidenfeld & Nicolson into one of Britain's leading publishing houses, whose lists reflect both his intellectual passions and his desire for history to be accurately recorded for future generations.

Weidenfeld studied law at Vienna University and foreign affairs at the Diplomatic Konsular Akademie, before emigrating to Britain to escape from Nazi Germany in 1938. He worked as a news commentator for the BBC Overseas Service during World War Two, during which time he conceived the idea of a magazine which would 'capture and perpetuate the European spirit of wartime London'. Assisted by Andre Deutsch, who was also to become a respected publisher, he established the Contacts Magazines and Book Company in 1945 and, in a bid to overcome the problem of post-war paper rationing, published the magazine, *Contact*, as a hardcover, as well as their first book, *New Deal For Coal*, by Harold Wilson, then a statistician in the Ministry of Fuel and Power.

He teamed up with Nigel Nicolson and in 1948, set up Weidenfeld & Nicolson, launching their first list a year later. An active Zionist, keen to be politically involved in the newly-formed State of Israel, Weidenfeld left Britain in 1949 to work as Political Advisor and Chef de Cabinet to Israel's first President, Dr. Chaim Weizmann. He returned in 1950 and in the ensuing years established a reputation for publishing the memoirs of some of the most significant political statesmen of the day, such as Moshe Dayan, Golda Meir and Yitzak Rabin. He commissioned work by eminent biographers and historians Elizabeth Longford, Antonia Fraser and Eric Hobsbawm, and published novelists such as Saul Bellow, Mary McCarthy, Heinrich Böll, Edna O'Brien and Margaret Drabble. In 1955 he caused a sensation by publishing *Lolita*, then seen as a scandalous text, today revered as one of the great literary classics of the 20th century.

Weidenfeld's contacts with world statesmen generated through his diplomatic work led to the securing of the memoirs of General de Gaulle and Konrad Adenauer, and those of President Lyndon Johnson and Henry Kissinger, to name but a few. Knighted in 1969 and made a Life Peer in 1976, he holds high German, French and Austrian decorations. He is an Honorary Senator of Bonn University, Honorary Fellow of St. Peter's and St. Anne's Colleges, Oxford, and Chairman of the Board of Governors of Ben-Gurion University of the Negev, Israel.

I count myself in nothing else so happy
As in a soul rememb'ring my good friends...
Henry Bolingbroke, Act II, Scene III, *Richard II*, by William Shakespeare

Main photograph: 17th April 1998, London
Inset photograph: Aged 8, dressed for a school play rehearsal

TREVOR MCDONALD

Sir Trevor McDonald OBE
Born 1939, Trinidad

News and current affairs journalist Trevor McDonald became a household name as the main anchorman of ITN's flagship news programme, *News at Ten*, from 1992 to 1999, and will forever be associated with the distinctive chimes of Big Ben that heralded its 10pm headlines.

Educated in Trinidad, McDonald began working in newspapers before moving into radio, becoming a news reader, continuity announcer, disc jockey and sports commentator. In 1962 he made his television debut presenting a nightly news programme and a current affairs show on Trinidad and Tobago Television.

He moved to London in 1969, becoming a producer for the Caribbean Service and World Service at BBC Radio, and four years later became an on-screen reporter with Independent Television News (ITN), covering domestic stories and reporting extensively from Northern Ireland. In 1978 he became a sports correspondent, covering the World Cup of that year, and by 1980 he had progressed to Diplomatic Correspondent, working on major stories in the Middle East, the U.S. and Europe. In 1982 he joined the fledgling Channel Four News programme and was appointed Diplomatic Editor in 1987.

McDonald established his reputation as a newscaster in 1989, when he became a presenter of *Channel Four News* and the early evening news on ITV, before taking the helm as the sole presenter of ITN's *News at Ten* in 1992. During his time with ITN he achieved a number of notable reporting coups: he was the first man to interview Nelson Mandela after his release from prison in 1990 and was the only British television journalist to interview Saddam Hussein, also in that year.

Controversial re-scheduling of ITV's news programming saw the final broadcast of *News at Ten* on 5th March 1999, with McDonald presiding over the launch, three days later, of ITN's *The Evening News* programme for ITV at 6.30pm. On 8th April, he began his own weekly, hour-long current affairs programme for ITN, *Tonight with Trevor McDonald*.

The recipient of numerous honorary degrees, McDonald was awarded the OBE in 1992 and was knighted in 1999.

For it is not true that the work of man is finished
that we have nothing more to do
but be parasites in the world
that all we need do now is keep in step with the world.
The work of man is only just beginning
and it remains to conquer
all the violence entrenched
in the recesses of his passion.
No race holds the monopoly of beauty, of intelligence, of strength
and there is a place for us all at the rendezvous of victory.
From *Return to My Native Land*, by Aimé Césaire, 1939

Main photograph: 1st February 1999, ITN newsroom, London
Inset photograph: Aged 19, Trinidad

KEN LOACH

Ken Loach
Born 1936. Nuneaton. Warwickshire

One of Britain's best and most controversial film-makers, Ken Loach is a director whose unwavering socialist convictions have fashioned his prestigious output for over 30 years. A pioneer of gritty, social realism in drama in the 1960s, his work is renowned for its naturalistic style and its commitment to voicing the struggles of the ordinary man.

A law graduate from Oxford University, Loach began work as an actor in repertory theatre before joining the BBC as a trainee in the drama department in 1963. He directed his first television play, *Diary of a Young Man*, in 1964 and began working on the Wednesday Play series in 1965, forming life-long collaborative partnerships with writers Jim Allen and Barry Hines, and producer Tony Garnett. In 1966 the transmission of the ground-breaking docu-drama, *Cathy Come Home*, a powerful depiction of homelessness, established an observational, documentary style of directing that was to be much imitated by his peers. Raw and hard-hitting, it had a significant impact on housing law and helped to launch the charity, Shelter.

Loach directed his first feature film, *Poor Cow*, in 1966 and two years later directed *Kes*, based on Hines's novel about a young Barnsley boy who cares for and trains a kestrel. The film explored society's failure to recognise the potential of every person and the confines it imposes on many working-class people, which were to become recurrent themes of Loach's drama, and established him as a major force in British cinema. During the next two decades he directed powerful feature films, such as *Looks and Smiles* (1981), and contentious television drama series, such as *Days of Hope* (1975), but the mood of the 80s was hostile to overtly political work, and his 1983 documentary series, *Questions of Leadership*, which was critical of the right-wing trade union leaders, was banned from transmission.

Loach's ability to generate startlingly authentic performances from often untutored actors attracted a wider cinema audience and critical acclaim for his feature films in the 90s, and international awards were bestowed upon *Hidden Agenda* (1990), *Riff-Raff* (1991), *Raining Stones* (1993), *Ladybird, Ladybird* (1994), *Land and Freedom* (1995) and *Carla's Song* (1996). His 1998 film, *My Name is Joe*, starring Peter Mullan, won the Best Actor award at the Cannes Film Festival and Best Picture at the British Independent Film Awards. Loach is the recipient of two lifetime achievement awards, from the Venice Film Festival in 1994 and the British Film Industry in 1999.

If society is to change for the better, then it will come from those who have most to gain from the change, it won't come from those at the top. And those who have most to gain can only have strength if they act together... If we are to get out of this mess, then it has to be by collective action, by people who have nothing to lose.

Main photograph: 3rd July 1998, Soho, London
Inset photograph: Aged 17

FREDERICK SANGER

Dr Frederick Sanger OM, CH, CBE, FRS
Born 1918, Rendcombe, Gloucestershire

Biochemist Frederick Sanger is one of only four scientists in the world to have been awarded the Nobel Prize twice. The first scientist to reveal the complete structure of a protein, he went on to develop one of the first techniques for reading the genetic code, engineering two revolutions in biology which are having a significant impact on modern medicine.

Sanger studied natural sciences at Cambridge University and, after obtaining his PhD in 1943, continued his research there, embarking on a 10-year project to determine the chemical structure of the protein insulin. Aware that the chemistry of proteins depended on the order in which their amino-acids were arranged, he tried to establish a technique for deducing the sequence. He devised many processes of protein analysis, such as the method of labelling protein fragments and, after painstaking research, succeeded in determining the complete structure of insulin in 1955. Awarded the Nobel Prize for Chemistry in 1958, Sanger has enabled chemists to synthesise insulin artificially, thus aiding diabetes sufferers, and has stimulated research into this vital field.

In 1962 he joined the Laboratory of Molecular Biology at the Research Council in Cambridge and began to focus on methods to determine the base sequences of DNA (deoxyribonucleic acid), the molecule that stores the genetic code of all living things. His research involved developing new techniques to split the DNA into different-sized fragments, after which they could be labelled, separated and comprehensively 'read'. In 1975 he pioneered an entirely new technique, known as the dideoxy method, for rapidly sequencing DNA, and by 1977 he had successfully determined the order of nucleotides in the DNA of the virus Phi X174. He shared the Nobel Prize for this work with Walter Gilbert of Harvard University and Paul Berg of Stanford University in 1980.

Sanger retired in 1983, his achievements having laid the groundwork for the vast, multi-national programme known as The Human Genome Project, which was established in the early 1990s to determine the sequence of the 70-100,000 genes that constitute the blueprint of a human being. An ambitious undertaking which will pioneer medical advances across the board, the project is taking place at Europe's leading human genome research institute, The Sanger Centre, which was founded in Cambridge in 1993.

We are DNA, but what else am I, and how do I know that I am, and what else are you?

Main photograph: 28th June 1999, Swaffham Bulbeck, Cambridge
Inset photograph: Aged 7

GEORGE BEST

George Best
Born 1946, Belfast, Northern Ireland

Hailed as 'the greatest footballer in the world' during his glory days for Manchester United, soccer virtuoso George Best dominated British football throughout the 1960s. An attacking winger, his speed, balance and snake-like dribbling skills were a compelling combination that resulted in phenomenal goal-scoring on the pitch and pop-star adulation off it.

Obsessed by football from the start, the skinny 13-year-old Best had passers-by pausing to watch his grace and skill as he teased a ball around the back streets of his council estate home. In 1961, on a tip-off from a family friend, the Northern Ireland scout for Manchester United watched him play in a local match. The same evening, the scout sent a telegram back to England, stating simply, 'I have found a genius', and the 15-year-old was dispatched to Old Trafford.

Best made his football league debut for United's first team against West Bromwich Albion in 1963, aged just 17, and in the same year, earned the first of his 31 caps for Northern Ireland. He won his first championship medal in the 1964-65 season and his second the following year, joining United's formidable front line-up of Bobby Charlton and Denis Law. By now an international celebrity, Best's display of skill against Benefica, Spain, in 1968, led United to victory in the European Cup, the first time an English club had ever won the championship, and earned him the title of the youngest ever European Footballer of the Year.

Dubbed 'the fifth Beatle', Best's looks, talent and showmanship were unrivalled, but the hard-drinking and late-night partying that accompanied this period in the 20-year-old's life began to take its toll. By 1971, lack of self-discipline and alcohol addiction led to widely publicised feuds with managers and numerous walk-outs before his eventual departure from United in 1974. Best played briefly for US soccer team The Los Angeles Aztecs in 1975, and returned to play two seasons with Fulham from 1976-78 but, unable to maintain peak form, played his last match with third division AFC Bournemouth in April 1983.

In spite of his premature demise, George Best's reputation as one of the most gifted footballers Britain has ever produced remains intact.

We kicked a ball around at every opportunity, from dawn till dusk. We did it because we loved it, but also because in those days there was nothing else for kids to do. There was very little football on television and there were no computer games, so when it was playtime, all you had was a kickabout in the street. After school we'd play again, usually until bedtime. My parents had to come looking for me every night. As soon as it got dark, all the other kids were being called in by their mums and dads all over the estate. Even when it was pitch black I'd still be there, smashing a ball against those garage doors.

MARY QUANT

Mary Quant OBE
Born 1934, London

Style icon of the 'Swinging Sixties', Mary Quant is the designer whose striking, geometric fashions liberated a generation of young women from the straitjackets that had restrained their mothers decades earlier. Famous for promoting the 'mini' skirt and creating easy-to-wear, loose-flowing tops, she brought the glamour of the catwalk to the high street, and introduced mass merchandising and the cult of the designer label.

Graduating from Goldsmiths College of Art in 1953, Quant designed hats for a leading milliner before opening a small boutique in the King's Road, London, with her future husband, Alexander Plunket Greene. Named *Bazaar*, it became the launching pad for a fashion revolution as Quant began to design specifically for the youth market. Raising hemlines and eyebrows, her trademark collections of mini-skirts, sleeveless crocheted tops, skinny-rib sweaters, coloured tights and low-slung hip belts, an ensemble dubbed 'The Chelsea Look,' were an instant hit and became the uniform of a generation. A second shop was opened in Knightsbridge in 1957, and six years later the Mary Quant Ginger Group was formed to manufacture clothing for worldwide distribution.

Awarded the OBE in 1966, Quant launched the Mary Quant cosmetics range to accompany her designs, which by then included rainwear, hosiery, underwear, swimwear and dress patterns. Her third *Bazaar* shop opened in Bond Street in 1967, and she expanded her range to incorporate hats (1967), household furnishings (1970), bedwear (1972) and even a doll called Daisy (1972). In 1973 the London Museum mounted a retrospective of her work, and in 1983 she launched ranges in Japan and opened the first Mary Quant Colour Shop in London, which has since grown into an international chain.

The woman who once declared that 'good taste is death' received the British Council Award for her contribution to the British fashion industry in 1990. The first Mary Quant Colour Concept Shop opened on Madison Avenue, New York in 1998 and the famous daisy logo, which began its career as a Quant doodle, is now a coveted status symbol adorning everything from nail polish to bedwear.

I grew up in a state of continual embarrassment because of the way I was dressed. I still remember every dress I had as a child. I hated them all except the few I managed, surreptitiously, to alter. I hated being forced to wear my cousin's cast-off clothes which were much too ornate for me. When I was about six and in bed with measles, I spent one night cutting up the bedspread – a sort of family heirloom that belonged to an aunt – with nail scissors. Even at that age I could see that the wild colour of the bedspread would make a super dress.

ANTHONY POWELL

Anthony Powell CH, CBE
Born 1905, London

Veteran British novelist Anthony Powell is best known for his 12-volume sequence of novels, *A Dance to the Music of Time*, a panoramic and satirical chronicle of the lives of the English middle and upper classes during the 20th century.

Educated at Oxford University, Powell worked in publishing and journalism before writing his first book, *Afternoon Men*, in 1931. A witty novel based in a hedonistic, party-loving London, it was followed by, amongst others, *Venusberg* (1932) and *What's Become of Waring?* (1939). After serving in the Welch Regiment and Intelligence Corps during World War Two, he published two works on the 17th century scholar John Aubrey and began contributing book reviews to *The Daily Telegraph*, in an association that was to continue for 30 years.

He embarked on his epic series *A Dance to the Music of Time* in 1951, opening with the novel *A Question of Upbringing*. Eleven books followed, including *At Lady Molly's* (1957), which won the James Tait Black Memorial Prize, and *Temporary Kings* (1973), winner of the W.H.Smith Prize, and the series concluded with *Hearing Secret Harmonies* in 1975. The cycle is framed through the eyes of the narrator, Nicholas Jenkins, whose generation, like Powell's, grew up in the shadow of the First World War, only to have their lives dislocated by the Second. Suffused with humour and melancholy, the broad sweep of narrative is set against the background of a fading England and throws up the power-crazed Kenneth Widmerpool, one of the most memorable characters of 20th-century fiction.

Powell published his memoirs in four volumes from 1976 to 1982, under the general title *To Keep the Ball Rolling*, and went on to produce the novels *O, How the Wheel Becomes It!* (1983) and *The Fisher King* (1986), two volumes of criticism, *Miscellaneous Verdicts* (1990) and *Under Review* (1992), and *Journals 1982-6* (1995). Thirty years after publication, *Afternoon Men* was adapted for the stage, and in 1997 Channel Four televised *A Dance to the Music of Time*.

Powell was awarded a CBE in 1956 and became a Companion of Honour in 1988.

'Virtue itself 'scapes not calumnious strokes,
The canker galls the infants of the spring...'
Laertes, Act I, Scene III, *Hamlet*, **by William Shakespeare**

DENIS HEALEY

The Rt. Hon. Lord Healey of Riddlesden in the County of West Yorkshire CH. MBE
Born 1917, Keighley, Yorkshire

The quintessential Labour heavyweight, former Chancellor of the Exchequer and widely respected intellectual, Denis Healey has been a dominant figure in politics throughout the latter half of the century.

Educated at Oxford University, where he obtained a double first in classics, Healey served with the Royal Engineers in North Africa and Italy during World War Two, where he attained the rank of major. He became Secretary of the International Department of the Labour Party (1945-52), gaining early experience in foreign affairs, before becoming MP for Leeds South East in 1952. He was appointed Secretary of State for Defence in Harold Wilson's government in 1964 and served as opposition spokesman on foreign affairs (1970-72) and treasury matters (1971-74) during the brief Tory reign.

A canny operator on the centre right of the party, Healey was appointed Chancellor of the Exchequer following Labour's return to power in 1974. He presided over a stormy period marked by a sterling crisis and the subsequent intervention of the International Monetary Fund, a humiliation which triggered a noisy clash with left-wingers at Labour's annual party conference, an event which haunted Labour for a generation. He failed to win the party leadership contests of 1976 and 1980, but was elected deputy leader in 1981, defeating his left-wing opponent, Tony Benn, by a small majority in a vigorously fought contest. He held the post of Shadow Foreign Secretary until 1987, when he resigned from the shadow cabinet.

Admired for his knowledge of foreign affairs, which in his heyday was considered unparalleled, Healey was made a Life Peer in 1992. An esteemed essayist, he has published several books and collections, and his autobiography, *The Time of My Life*, was the bestselling political memoir in 1991.

He who binds to himself a joy
Does the winged life destroy,
But he who kisses the joy as it flies
Lives in eternity's sun rise.
From *Eternity*, by William Blake (1757-1827)

Main photograph: 23rd November 1996, Alfriston, East Sussex
Inset photograph: Aged 5

PETER BENENSON

Peter Benenson
Born 1921, London

Peter Benenson is the lawyer who founded Amnesty International, the biggest human rights organisation in the world, which has assisted in the release of thousands of torture victims and prisoners of conscience since its inception in 1961.

The son of Jewish parents, Benenson was educated at Eton where, aged just 16, he launched a campaign to help victims of fascism in Spain, organising school support for the newly formed Spanish Relief Committee which aided Republican children orphaned by the war. A year later, while still at school, he campaigned to assist Jews fleeing Nazi Germany and raised a colossal £4,000 to bring two young German Jews to Britain.

Benenson served in the Ministry of Information during World War Two before graduating from Oxford Univeristy. He went on to study law and specialised in representing victims of injustice. His decision to dedicate his life to fighting for human rights was prompted by an item in *The Daily Telegraph* in November 1960, about the seven-year imprisonment of two Portuguese students who had been 'caught' drinking a toast to liberty in a Lisbon café. Horrified by the tyranny, Benenson gathered support from a group of lawyer friends and launched the Appeal for Amnesty 1961, a year-long campaign for the release of political prisoners worldwide. His manifesto, *The Forgotten Prisoners*, was published in *The Observer* and newspapers across Europe on 28 May 1961 and attracted overwhelming support.

Establishing a neutral political stance, he devised the 'Groups of Three' system whereby small local groups of supporters 'adopt' three prisoners, people who have been falsely imprisoned or tortured or who face the death penalty, in different parts of the world and write letters to jailers, heads of government and embassies, pleading for the prisoners' freedom and effectively embarrassing them into action. Notifying oppressive governments that they were being monitored in this manner was a revolutionary and successful way of exerting moral pressure, and within a year groups were established in nine European countries and Amnesty International was officially founded. Awarded the Nobel Peace prize in 1977, Amnesty currently operates in 44 countries worldwide.

A man who is free is a man without fear. The greatest battle is the fight against fear. Freedom to live without fear, in dignity, and to speak or worship without reprisals are the concern not of one culture but of the entire human race.

Main photograph: 5th February 1999, Oxford
Inset photograph: Aged 8

V.S. NAIPAUL

Sir Vidiadhar Surajprasad Naipaul
Born 1932, Chaguanas, Trinidad

Novelist V.S. Naipaul is regarded as a unique and powerful voice in contemporary literature. His body of work focuses primarily on themes of nationality and identity, political upheaval and displacement, and is widely admired for its insightful portrayal of the post-colonial experience.

Naipaul came to Britain in 1950 to study English at Oxford University. In 1955 he became editor of the BBC World Service radio series *Caribbean Voices* and worked as a journalist before publishing his first novel, *The Mystic Masseur*, in 1957. Set in his native Trinidad, it is a sympathetically satirical portrayal of Indian subculture in the West Indies. He continued this theme in his next three novels, *The Suffrage of Elvira* (1958), *Miguel Street* (1959) and *The House of Mr Biswas* (1961), and it was the latter, partly based on his father's life, which firmly established his literary credentials.

In 1971 he won the Booker prize for his novel, *In A Free State*, which explores issues of nationality through three linked narratives of displaced characters: a servant from Bombay transported to Washington, a lost and angry West Indian youth in London, and a white man and woman in a hostile African state. Further successes followed with *A Bend in the River* (1979), about life under an African dictator, and *The Enigma of Arrival* (1987), a depiction of a young Trinidadian's experience of post-imperial Britain. Naipaul's broad, intense experience of human nature is also reflected in his travel books and works of political journalism, such as *The Middle Passage* (1962), which focuses on the Caribbean, *An Area of Darkness* (1964), his highly controversial and critical account of India, *Among The Believers: an Islamic Journey* (1981) and *A Turn in the South* (1989), which centres on Evangelical Christianity in the southern states of the USA.

His recent works include the novel *A Way in the World* (1994) and the non-fiction *Beyond Belief: Islamic Excursions* (1998), which continue to explore themes of political violence, homelessness and alienation. A novelist and critic of societies, whose work has generated comparisons with Joseph Conrad and Henry James, Naipaul was knighted in 1990.

But already I had grown to live with the idea that things changed: already I lived with the idea of decay....Already I lived with the idea of death, the idea, impossible for a young person to possess, to hold in his heart, that one's time on earth, one's life, was a short thing. These ideas, of a world in decay, a world subject to constant change, and of the shortness of human life, made many things bearable.
From *The Enigma of Arrival*, by Naipaul, 1987

PAT ARROWSMITH

Pat Arrowsmith
Born 1930, Leamington Spa

Peace campaigner and socialist, Pat Arrowsmith has been an instrumental figure in non-violent, direct action campaigns over the past four decades, opposing nuclear weapons, the Vietnam War in the 70s and the Gulf War in the 90s. She has been imprisoned 11 times for anti-war civil disobedience and was twice adopted by Amnesty International as a prisoner of conscience.

Educated at Cambridge University, Ohio University and Liverpool University, Arrowsmith spent a year working in race-relations in Chicago before returning to Britain in 1954, where she trained as a social worker. She has been, briefly, a social worker in Liverpool and Plymouth and has held a variety of jobs from nursing assistant in a psychiatric hospital to Council gardener. Throughout her working life she has been an active trade unionist and, although not deeply involved in conventional politics, has three times been fielded as a general election candidate, standing on peace and socialist issues.

In 1957 Arrowsmith joined a group hoping to sail into the British H-Bomb testing zone at Christmas Island, and became a full-time peace and nuclear disarmament activist from about 1958-68. She was an organiser for the Direct Action Committee against Nuclear War and the Committee of 100, and was Organising Secretary of the first London-to-Aldermaston march in 1958. She helped to initiate, and participated in, two trans-national endeavours to take in-situ, non-violent, direct action, first against the Vietnam War and later against the 1991 Gulf War (1991), when she was a member of a war-zone peace camp and for which she was awarded a US Group's Peace Prize.

In 1971 she joined the Amnesty International staff, and remained on it for 24 years.

While engaged in anti-war activity in Britain, involving the encouragement of anti-nuclear industrial action and disaffection among the troops, Arrowsmith has had several novels and self-illustrated collections of poetry published. She has drawn and painted all her life, and occasionally exhibited her work.

'You never know anyone well enough'
A saying from her long-gone brother Peter

PATRICK MOORE

Patrick Moore CBE
Born 1923, Pinner, Middlesex

Leading astronomer Patrick Moore is best known as the presenter of *The Sky at Night*, the longest-running programme with the same presenter in British television history. A lunar cartographer whose pioneering work was integral to the historic 1969 moon landings, he is a prolific writer, and is credited with having popularised a niche science through his ability to capture the imagination of a lay audience.

Moore's passion for astronomy began after reading G.F. Chambers's *Story of the Solar System* when he was just six years old. Presented with a three-inch telescope when he was 11, he was able to view the stars from his bedroom window, and in the same year he became the youngest ever member of the British Astronomical Association. Educated privately at home due to ill-health, Moore qualified for a place at Cambridge University to study geology, but when war broke out in 1939, he decided to enlist. Lying about his age, he fiddled his medical and joined the RAF as a navigator in the Bomber Command.

In 1945 he set up a private observatory at East Grinstead and wrote his first book on astronomy, *Guide to The Moon*, rapidly making his name as an expert on lunar and planetary cartography and becoming an official moonmapper for NASA in 1946. On 24th April 1957, six months before the Russians launched Sputnik 1 and the start of the space race, he presented the first programme of a monthly, late-night BBC television series called *The Sky at Night*, where his enthusiastic commentary endeared him to a loyal audience.

In 1959 the Russians used Moore's painstakingly researched charts of the lunar surface to launch their first unmanned craft around the moon, sending the first satellite pictures of the dark side of the moon 'live' to his programme. Ten years later the Americans used them for the famous Apollo mission that put Neil Armstrong on the moon, and Moore led the BBC's coverage of the historic event. Awarded the OBE in 1968, he has since commentated on every major breakthrough and development in astronomy and space exploration.

President of the British Astronomical Association (1982-84), Moore became a star, literally, in 1982, when Minor Planet no. 2602, discovered by the Lowell Observatory, Arizona, was named after him. He was awarded the CBE in 1988, and has published widely throughout the 90s.

There's so much to learn. An astronomer once said to me: 'I thought I knew everything about the constitution of the stars in 1925. Then I knew less in 1930 and even less in 1935.' The more you know, you realise the less you know. Astronomy teaches us how insignificant we are. We ought to be rather more sensible.

Main photograph: 2nd February 1999, Selsey, Sussex
Inset photograph: Aged 17

JOHN MAJOR

The Rt. Hon. John Major CH, MP
Born John Major-Ball, 1943, Merton, London

The last Conservative Prime Minister of the 20th century, John Major is credited with bringing a steadiness to public life after the turbulence of the Thatcher years, and stewarding the first stages of the Northern Ireland peace process, which culminated in the Good Friday Agreement of 1998.

The son of a circus performer, Major left school at 16 and worked for the Standard Chartered Bank in Nigeria before becoming a local government councillor in Lambeth in 1968. He was elected the member for Huntingdonshire in Margaret Thatcher's victory of 1979 and became an assistant government whip and treasury whip between 1983 and 1985.

Appointed Secretary of State for Social Security in 1986 and then Chief Secretary to the Treasury in 1987, he became Foreign Secretary in 1989 and within months was appointed Chancellor of the Exchequer, engineering Britain's entry into the European exchange rate mechanism (ERM). Following Thatcher's enforced resignation during the 1990 Conservative party leadership contest, Major was her chosen successor and became Prime Minister. He made a favourable impression on the nation by his calm handling of the 1991 Gulf War with Iraq, his scrapping of the unpopular 'poll tax' and his conciliatory approach to Europe, signing the Treaty of Maastricht but postponing Britain's decision to join monetary union.

Re-elected in 1992, Major was forced to pull Britain out of the ERM after a desperate attempt to protect the weakening pound by raising interest rates had failed, but 'Black Wednesday' incurred a further plunge in value and the wrath of the anti-European faction of his party. His 1993 Downing Street Declaration with the Irish Premier Albert Reynolds, however, establishing the right of Northern Irish citizens to decide their political fate, led to a welcome ceasefire in the hostilities. Having stabilised the economy, Major was sullied by allegations of sleaze levelled at a number of his ministers, and continuing attacks by right-wing Eurosceptics led to his resignation and a leadership contest. He defeated John Redwood's challenge, remaining in Downing Street during the BSE, or 'mad cow disease', crisis of 1996, but resigned as leader after the Labour landslide of 1997.

Major was made a Companion of Honour in 1999 in recognition of his work towards the historic Northern Ireland peace agreement.

If you can talk with crowds and keep your virtue,
Or walk with Kings – nor lose the common touch,
If neither foes nor loving friends can hurt you,
If all men count with you, but none too much;
If you can fill the unforgiving minute
With sixty seconds' worth of distance run,
Yours is the Earth and everything that's in it,
And – which is more – you'll be a Man, my son!

From *If*, by Rudyard Kipling (1865-1936)

Main photograph: 28th January 1999, House of Commons, London
Inset photograph: Aged 9

BILL DEEDES

The Rt. Hon. Lord Deedes of Aldington in the County of Kent MC, DL
Born William Deedes, 1913, Hampstead, London

Journalist and former Tory MP, Bill Deedes has been a fixture in Fleet Street for nearly 70 years, covering world events that span the 1936 Abdication Crisis to the 1999 war in Kosovo. Known to many as the recipient of the fictitious letters from Denis Thatcher in *Private Eye* magazines's 'Dear Bill' column, and rumoured to be the model for Boot, the war correspondent in Evelyn Waugh's classic 1938 novel Scoop, he is widely respected for his commitment to press reporting.

Deedes began his career as a reporter for the *Morning Post* in 1931 and got his first big break when he was sent to cover the war in Abyssinia in 1935. He returned to London a year later to work as the Post's lobby correspondent at Westminster before joining *The Daily Telegraph* in 1937. He reported Munich in 1938, covering Neville Chamberlain's negotiations with Adolf Hitler, after which he served in the 12th King's Royal Rifles during World War Two, for which he won the Military Cross.

He returned to *The Daily Telegraph*'s Peterborough column in 1945, and in 1950, embarked on a parallel career in politics, becoming MP for Ashford, a seat he held for 24 years. He was appointed junior minister for housing in 1954, and transferred to the Home Office in Anthony Eden's government a year later. Deedes retired from office in 1957 when Harold Macmillan became Prime Minister but, in the wake of the Premier's 'night of the long knives' in 1962, returned as Minister Without Portfolio in charge of information, and oversaw the government's handling of the 1963 Profumo Scandal.

He resigned from Parliament in 1974 and was appointed editor of *The Daily Telegraph*, where he remained for 12 years. When Conrad Black became the paper's proprietor in 1986, Deedes was replaced as editor but stayed on as leader writer and took on a new role as columnist and reporter, aged 73. In 1986 he was made a Life Peer and in 1989, he became closely involved with CARE International, the largest aid and development organisation in the world, travelling the global war zones to report on the political environment and the organisation's work.

An active supporter of the Mines Advisory Group, Deedes was the only journalist to accompany Diana, the late Princess of Wales, on her trip to Bosnia in 1997 to raise awareness of the dangers of landmines.

We go this way only once, and there seems so little time in which to explore the world and its wonder, to find out more about the human tragedy – of which we are part. 'Never forget', the Austrian poet Rilke said to his wife as he lay dying, 'life is magnificent', and so it is. I believe there is a future life, but I do not let that discourage me from trying to get the most out of this one.

Main photograph: 28th June 1999, Canary Wharf, London
Inset photograph: As a schoolboy at Eton

MURIEL SPARK

Dame Muriel Spark
Born Muriel Sarah Camberg, 1918, Edinburgh

Novelist, poet, biographer, dramatist, short-story writer and critic, Muriel Spark is one of Britain's most distinguished authors. Celebrated for her witty and astute observations of the darker aspects of human nature, she has built a body of fiction based around themes of loyalty and betrayal, devotion and blackmail, and imbued with metaphysical and moral questions.

Spark was educated at James Gillespie's School for Girls, which she later used as the model for the Marcia Blaine School in her most famous novel, *The Prime of Miss Jean Brodie*, and at Heriot Watt College, Edinburgh. In 1947 she became General Secretary of the Poetry Society and edited the prestigious *Poetry Review*. She began to write full-time after winning *The Observer* short story competition in 1951 with *The Seraph and The Zambesi*, and published her first collection of poetry, *The Fanfarlo and Other Verse*, in 1952.

Spark converted to Roman Catholicism in 1954, and two years later published her first novel, the critically acclaimed *The Comforters* (1957), which was based on her observations of the paradoxes and ironies of the Catholic faith. She further established her literary position with *Memento Mori* (1959), *The Ballad of Peckham Rye* (1960) and *The Bachelors* (1961). It was her sixth novel, however, *The Prime of Miss Jean Brodie* (1961), that propelled her to international fame. The story of an emancipated school teacher whose progressive ideas have a devastating impact on her own and her pupils' lives, was an instant best-seller which was later adapted to a successful stage play in 1966 and a hit film in 1969.

Her novel *The Mandelbaum Gate* (1965) won the James Tait Black Memorial Prize, and further success followed with *The Abbess of Crewe* (1974), an allegorical fantasy satirising the Watergate scandal, *Territorial Rights* (1979), *Loitering With Intent* (1981), *The Only Problem* (1984) and *A Far Cry From Kensington* (1988). Created a Dame in 1993, Spark won the David Cohen British Literature Prize for a lifetime's achievement in 1997.

Relations with people are never finished, whereas with a book it's done. It's an illusion to think we can tie up all the loose ends.

PETER DE LA BILLIÈRE

General Sir Peter de la Billière KCB, KBE, DSO, MC, DL
Born 1934, Plymouth

One of the most highly decorated soldiers since the Second World War, Peter de la Billière ranks among our most distinguished military figures. As Commander of the SAS, he was operations director during the 1980 siege of the Iranian Embassy, and as Senior British Commander in the Gulf, he oversaw the largest deployment of British troops since World War Two.

The son of a Surgeon Lieutenant Commander who was killed in action in 1941, de la Billière, a self-confessed rebel and loner, joined the King's Shropshire Light Infantry in 1952, aged 17. Within weeks he had been selected for officer training and was soon commissioned into the Durham Light Infantry as a Second Lieutenant. He served in Korea, Japan and Egypt before joining the Special Air Service in 1956, fighting communist terrorists in Malaya, and won his first Military Cross after leading a troop assault on Jebel Akhdar in Oman in 1959.

He commanded A Squadron 22 SAS (1964-66) and as Commanding Officer (1972-74), oversaw action in Musandam and Dhofar, receiving a Distinguished Service Order in 1976. The following year, he commanded the British Army Training Team in Sudan, and between 1979 and 1983 he commanded the SAS Group, taking on the overall military command for the successful assault to release the hostages in the Iranian Embassy siege in London.

In 1982 de la Billière was put in charge of Special Forces Operations during the Falklands War, and was awarded a CBE in 1983. He served as Military Commissioner and Commander of the British Forces, Falkland Islands for a year in 1984, and after two years as General Officer Commanding Wales, he became GOC South East District and Permanent Peace Time Commander of Joint Forces Operations Staff in 1987. Awarded the KCB in 1988, he assumed command of the British Forces Middle East in 1990, and a year later led 45,000 British servicemen in Operation Desert Storm in the Gulf War. On his return to the UK, he was knighted a second time, promoted to General and became special advisor to the Ministry of Defence on Middle East matters.

De la Billière retired from active service in June 1992 and will be remembered for his principles of meticulous battle training and unwavering commitment to troop welfare.

'We are the Pilgrims, master: we shall go
Always a little farther: it may be
Beyond the last blue mountain barred with snow,
Across that angry or that glimmering sea'

From *The Golden Road to Samarkand*, by James Ellroy Flecker (1884-1915), inscribed on the clocktower in Hereford commemorating SAS members who have died in service since World War Two.

Main photograph: 2nd September 1998, London
Inset photograph: Aged 16

CAMERON MACKINTOSH

Sir Cameron Mackintosh
Born 1946, Enfield

The most successful theatre producer this century, Cameron Mackintosh has dominated London's West End and New York's Broadway for the past 30 years. Renowned for his entrepreneurial flair, he has produced a string of hit musicals which have revived the British musical tradition and achieved record runs worldwide.

The son of a semi-professional jazz musician, Mackintosh resolved to become a producer at the age of eight, after seeing his first musical, *Salad Days* (1954). In 1963 he enrolled at the Central School of Speech and Drama in London but left after a year to become assistant stage manager on the musical *Oliver*. Six years later, aged 23, he produced his first musical, Cole Porter's *Anything Goes*, and went on to produce several hit shows, most notably *Godspell*. In 1976 he had his first major international success with Stephen Sondheim's *Side By Side By Sondheim*, followed by sell-out productions of *My Fair Lady* and *Oklahoma!*

In 1980 his meeting with composer Andrew Lloyd Webber cemented one of the most successful collaborations in the history of musical theatre. Their first joint venture, *CATS*, opened in London in May 1981, and by February 1996 it had become the longest-running musical in the West End and by 1997 the longest-running show in Broadway history. Mackintosh's subsequent successes included *Song and Dance* and *Little Shop of Horrors*, but arguably his greatest triumph was in 1985 when, in collaboration with the French writing team of Alain Boublil and Claude-Michel Schonberg, his production of *Les Miserables* opened at London's Palace Theatre to rave reviews. The following year, working again with Lloyd Webber, he produced the hugely successful *Phantom of the Opera*, and in 1989, with Boublil and Schonberg again, he produced *Miss Saigon*.

In 1990 *Five Guys Named Moe* enjoyed a record run in London's West End and in 1992 Mackintosh opened a new production of *Carousel*. In 1994 his revised production of *Oliver* opened at the London Palladium and his third collaboration with Boublil and Schonberg, *Martin Guerre*, opened at the Prince Edward Theatre in 1996. In 1998 he took Matthew Bourne's stunning, all-male *Swan Lake* to Broadway and produced the Sondheim show, *Putting it Together*.

Mackintosh was knighted for services to British theatre in 1996.

If I start looking behind me
And begin retracing my track
I'll remind you to remind me
We said we wouldn't look back
From *Salad Days*, by Julian Slade and Dorothy Reynolds, 1954

JAMES CALLAGHAN

The Rt. Hon. Lord Callaghan of Cardiff
Born 1912, Portsmouth

Labour elder statesman and former Prime Minister, James Callaghan holds the distinction of being the only British politician to have held all the major offices of state in his 43-year political career.

Callaghan worked for the Inland Revenue from the age of 17 before becoming a union official in 1933. He served in the Navy during the Second World War and was elected Labour MP for Cardiff South in the 1945 General Election. A centrist by instinct, he rose swiftly through the ranks of opposition and was appointed Shadow Chancellor by Hugh Gaitskell in 1961. In 1963 he stood for the leadership of the party but was defeated by his great rival, Harold Wilson. Following Labour's 1964 election victory he served as Chancellor of the Exchequer but resigned in 1967 in a dispute with Wilson over the devaluation of sterling. A skilful communicator, he was appointed Home Secretary in 1967, winning plaudits for his pragmatism and calm handling of the 1969 Troubles in Northern Ireland. When Labour returned to power in 1974, after the brief Tory interregnum, he became Foreign Secretary.

In 1976 Callaghan was chosen by Labour MPs to become Prime Minister after Wilson's unexpected resignation, and he played an impressive role in the development of the international politics of detente. He negotiated the 'Lib-Lab pact' with the Liberal Party, in a bid to ensure the government's survival, but failed to gain either party or union support for his anti-inflation policies, and the infamous 'Winter of Discontent' of 1978-79 saw the government locked in battle with the major trade unions, while the country hovered on the brink of chaos. Deciding against calling a General Election in the autumn of 1978, Callaghan received a vote of no confidence in March 1979. The Conservatives came to power under Margaret Thatcher in the subsequent election and the following year, Michael Foot took over as leader of the opposition.

In 1987 Callaghan was created a Life Peer and published his autobiography, *Time and Chance*.

Come, my friends.
'Tis not too late to seek a newer world.
Push off, and sitting well in order smite
The sounding furrows; for my purpose holds
To sail beyond the sunset, and the baths
Of all the western stars, until I die.
From *Ulysses*, by Alfred Lord Tennyson, 1842

Professor Watson, born 1928, Chicago, USA
Professor Crick OM, FRS born 1916, Northampton, England
Professor Wilkins CBE, FRS born 1916, New Zealand

Watson, Crick and Wilkins shared the 1962 Nobel Prize for Physiology or Medicine for the greatest biological discovery of the 20th century, the unravelling of the structure of DNA, the chemical blueprint for life.

Biophysicist Crick joined the Medical Research Council's group at the University of Cambridge's Cavendish Laboratory in 1949 and teamed up with American biochemist Watson in 1951. The pair began studying the structure of the deoxyribonucleic acid (DNA) molecule, which transmits genetic characteristics from one generation to the next, Crick using his knowledge of X-ray diffraction and Watson his understanding of phage and bacterial genetics.

Assisted by X-ray diffraction images of DNA produced by biophysicist Wilkins, based at King's College, London, and X-ray crystallographer, the late Rosalind Franklin, they were able to build a 3-D model of DNA that revealed its 'double helix' structure, two intertwined, helically-coiled chains resembling a spiral ladder, the rails of which are made of alternating units of phosphate and the sugar deoxyribose, the rungs composed of a pair of nitrogen-containing nucleotides. Their 1953 discovery provided a massive advance in the field of genetics and launched the molecular biological revolution.

Crick continued to study genetic coding and the mechanism of protein synthesis, research which has paved the way for the modern industries of biotechnology, genetic finger-printing and screening for inherited diseases. He relocated to the Salk Institute in San Diego, California in 1977 and turned his attention to brain research.

Watson returned to the USA and became Professor of Biology at Harvard in 1961. He was Director of Cold Spring Harbour Laboratory in New York from 1964 to 1994, when he was made President, and served as Director of the National Center For Human Genome Research (1989-92). Wilkins was Professor of Molecular Biology at King's College, London (1963-70), and then Professor of Biophysics (1970-80). He was Director of the Medical Research Council Cell Biophysics Unit (1974-80) and President of the British Society for Social Responsibility in Science (1969-91).

DNA has been around for at least several billion years. If we hadn't discovered the double-helix when we did, someone else would have done soon after. As the painter John Minton once said, 'The important thing is to be there when the picture is painted.' And this, it seems to me, is partly a matter of luck and good judgement, partly inspiration and application.
Francis Crick

TANNI GREY

Tanni Grey MBE
Born 1969, Cardiff

Tanni Grey is one of Britain's leading Paralympic athletes, whose wheelchair racing has earned her a colossal 24 world records and nine gold medals. In addition to her inspirational performances on the track, she has won plaudits for her dedication to raising the profile of the Paralympic Games and her fight for equal opportunities for the disabled.

Born with spina bifida, Grey became a wheelchair user from the age of eight, but had a passion for sport, playing basketball and tennis, and enjoying horse-riding, swimming and archery. Educated in Glamorgan, she took PE lessons at a neighbouring school where she won her first wheelchair race on sports day and became hooked on competing. She netted a string of trophies at inter-school matches and secured a place in the Welsh team for the British Sports Association Junior National Games at Stoke Mandeville in 1981. Aged only 12, she took the gold in the girls' junior slalom and won a silver medal in the 100 metres.

Competing in both local and national events, she set a new British record in the 100m at the 1984 Stoke Mandeville Games and came first in the wheelchair slalom at the 1986 British Paraplegic Games. In 1987 she began a degree course in politics at Loughborough University and combined top-level training with her studies. She began to compete internationally, and won a bronze medal in the 1988 Seoul Olympics.

In 1992 she won a staggering four gold medals at the Barcelona Paralympic Games, for the 100, 200, 400 and 800 metre events, and went on to win eight medals at the World Championships between 1993 and 1995. At the 1996 Paralympic Games in Atlanta she seized another gold for the 800m, setting a new world record time of 1:53:35, and three silver medals. In 1998 she won gold for the 800m Exhibition event at the European Championships and gold for the 200m at the World Championships.

An authority on disability sporting issues, Grey regularly appears on radio and television, and was awarded an MBE in 1994. Vice-President of the Women's Sports Foundation and patron of the Youth Sports Trust, she works part-time for UK Athletics and was appointed a member of the United Kingdom Sports Council in 1998.

'Aim high, even if you hit a cabbage.'
Advice from her grandfather

YEHUDI MENUHIN

Lord Menuhin of Stoke d'Abernon in the County of Surrey OM
Born 1916, New York

Yehudi Menuhin is universally acknowledged as the foremost violinist of the age, a child prodigy who made his debut in San Francisco aged seven, and in whose life the history of 20th-century music is mirrored. A humanitarian and educator, committed to fighting prejudice and oppression, he put his prodigious musical skills to the service of mankind for over 75 years.

Born into a Russian Jewish family of distinguished musicians, the child Menuhin first studied with Louis Persinger of the San Francisco Symphony Orchestra before moving to Paris in 1926 to study with the Romanian violinist, Georges Enesco. At the age of 12, his performance of concertos by Bach, Beethoven and Brahms in Berlin in 1929 caused a sensation, inspiring audience member Albert Einstein to declare, 'Now I know there is a God in heaven'. Musical history was made three years later when the 16-year-old performed Edward Elgar's concerto at the Royal Albert Hall, conducted by the ageing composer himself. Acclaimed for his technical brilliance and extraordinary maturity of interpretation, Menuhin completed his first world tour in 1935 and went on to play over 500 concerts for the allied forces in Europe, America and the Pacific during World War Two.

A passionate believer that music was a force for peace, Menuhin played to concentration camp survivors in Germany after the end of the war, and in 1950 he disregarded assassination threats to play in the newly-created State of Israel. Having settled in England, he set up the Gstaad Festival in 1956, began conducting and formed his own chamber orchestra in 1958. In 1963 he founded the celebrated Yehudi Menuhin School of Music for gifted pupils, where violin, viola, cello and piano are still taught. A lover of a wide range of musical influences, he famously duetted with French jazz musician Stephane Grappelli and played in Indian raga with the sitar player Ravi Shankar, bridging the gap between the classics and jazz, and broadening the boundaries of musical appreciation.

A collaborator with Bartok and Toscanini, befriended by Sibelius and Shostakovich, Menuhin will be remembered for his definitive recordings of the Beethoven and Elgar violin concertos. The recipient of multiple honours, including the Croix de Lorraine from General de Gaulle and the Nehru Award for International Understanding, he was created a Life Peer in 1993. Lord Menuhin died in March 1999, aged 82, whilst on a concert tour of Germany.

At the age of four I was too young to know that the violin would exact a price commensurate with the grace it conferred – the grace of flying, of occupying an absolute vantage point, of enjoying such dominion over nerve, bone and muscle as could render the body an ecstatic absentee. But I did know, instinctively, that to play was to be.

SEAMUS HEANEY

Seamus Heaney
Born 1939, County Derry, Northern Ireland

Nobel prize-winning poet Seamus Heaney is widely regarded as one of the most influential writers of the 20th century. An Irish Catholic, loyal to the English literary tradition, he is revered for his masterful command of language and the earthiness of his verse, which focuses largely on Irish history and the Northern Ireland Troubles.

A farmer's son, Heaney was one of the first Catholic boys to win a scholarship to Queen's College, Belfast, graduating in 1961. He lectured at St Joseph's College of Education and became a key figure in Philip Hobsbaum's Belfast writers group, making his debut as a poet with *Eleven Poems* published in 1965. A year later he achieved international recognition for his first collection of poems, *Death of a Naturalist*, which won numerous prizes including the Somerset Maugham Award. This work, followed by *Door into the Dark* (1969), drew heavily upon his rural upbringing to express a central theme of his later work, the need to dig down through history and language to unearth the primal sources of the self.

Appointed lecturer in English at Queen's College in 1966, Heaney resigned following the Bloody Sunday riots in January 1972 and moved to the Republic, taking Irish citizenship. His subsequent poetry, such as *Wintering Out* (1972), which reflected upon the outbreak of sectarian violence in Ulster in 1969, and *North* (1975), his most highly acclaimed volume, sought to unearth the roots of the tribal and religious conflict and to explore the role of language and its relation to politics and history. These poems, together with those in *Field Work* (1979), led to Heaney being recognised as the most important Irish poet since W.B.Yeats.

During the 1980s he explored more personal and spiritual themes in collections such as *Station Island* (1984), *The Haw Lantern* (1987) and *Seeing Things* (1991). Heaney has been Boylston Professor of Rhetoric and Oratory at Harvard since 1985 and Professor of Poetry at Oxford University since 1989, and is also a leading literary critic and essayist. Awarded the Nobel Peace Prize for Literature in 1995, his collection of poetry, *Spirit Level*, won the Whitbread Prize in 1997. He published *Opened Ground: Poems 1966-1994* in 1998 and his translation of *Beowulf* in 1999.

Heaviness of being. And poetry
Sluggish in the doldrums of what happens.
Me waiting until I was nearly fifty
To credit marvels. Like the tree-clock of tin-cans
The tinkers made. So long for air to brighten.
Time to be dazzled and the heart to lighten.
From *Fosterling*, published in *Seeing Things*, 1991

Main photograph: 7th September 1998, London
Inset photograph: Aged 27, Belfast

NORMAN WISDOM

Norman Wisdom. OBE
Born 1915. Paddington. London

Norman Wisdom is one of television's earliest comedy stars, a slapstick genius famous for his hapless grin, ill-fitting suits and tweed cap turned up at the peak. An actor and performer, he developed his gormless, accident-prone alter-ego 'Norman' in post-war music hall shows and has built a 60-year career brilliantly playing the fool.

After a troubled childhood, Wisdom joined the army as a band boy in the 10th Hussars at the age of 14 and taught himself to play the clarinet, saxophone and trumpet. When war broke out in 1939 he was transferred to the Royal Corps of Signals and began to develop his natural comic talent, entertaining the troops with acts featuring slapstick falls and acrobatics. He made his stage debut in a variety show at Collins Music Hall in 1945 and after numerous appearances in pantomime and revues, made his West End debut at the London Casino in 1948. In the same year he appeared in the variety show *Out of the Blue* at the Spa Theatre, Scarborough where, in addition to his 12-minute speciality act, he introduced the hapless, scruffy 'Norman', who would emerge as a volunteer from the audience to 'wreck' colleague David Nixon's magic act. His madcap antics made him a household name and he went on to star in the BBC television series *Rooftop Rendezvous* as well as making his film debut in *A Date With a Dream* (1948).

Wisdom appeared in his first Royal Variety Performance in 1952, and a year later landed his own television series *It's Norman*. In 1954 he won an Academy Award and international acclaim for his lead role in the film farce, *Trouble in Store*, where he famously caused chaos in a department store. Numerous screen appearances followed over the next 18 years, notably in *Man of the Moment* (1955), *There Was a Crooked Man* (1960), and *A Stitch in Time* (1963) and he appeared on Broadway in 1966 in *Walking Happy*, a musical version of *Hobson's Choice*. In 1968 he was nominated for Best Supporting Actor for his role in the hit comedy film *The Night They Raided Minsky's* and returned to the small screen in the BBC series *Norman* in 1970. Further situation comedies such as *Nobody is Norman Wisdom* and *A Little Bit of Wisdom* followed in 1973, and in 1981 he won plaudits for his first 'straight' role, portraying a dying cancer patient in the BAFTA award-winning television play *Going Gently*.

Wisdom toured throughout the 90s, performing in *The Legendary Norman Wisdom – Live on Stage*, and was awarded the OBE in 1995.

Such is life
And life is such
And after all
It isn't much
First a cradle, then a hearse
It might have been better
But it could have been worse!

Main photograph: 23rd April 1998. London
Inset photograph: Aged 14

JOHN HORDER

Dr. John Horder CBE, FRCP, FRCPE, FRCGP, FRCPsych.
Born 1919, Ealing, London

John Horder is credited with elevating general practice to new levels of academic excellence and prestige within the professions concerned with health and social care.

Horder studied medicine at Oxford University after first reading classics there, and completed his clinical training at the London Hospital in 1948. He intended to pursue a career in psychiatry but took a short locum job in a general practice in 1951. Realising that he had inadvertently found his vocation, he went on to become a GP in north London. In 1952 he joined the newly-founded College of General Practitioners, which was established to raise the profile of general medical practice through education and research, fields from which it had previously been excluded.

Working in various capacities in the College headquarters, Horder emerged as a strategic thinker and theorist during the 1960s. He argued for a different balance between the physical aspects, hitherto dominant, and the psychological and social aspects of medical practice. In 1960 he was the first GP to be appointed as a consultant to the World Health Organisation, working with a committee concerned with the role of GPs and Public Health Officers.

Frustrated by the medical profession's then disparaging view of general practice and convinced that it should be seen and valued as an equal partner with the specialties, to all of which it was an essential complement, he was a key figure in the College's campaign to introduce a special training for this role, to begin after qualification as a doctor. This was essential if the standard of health care was to improve and young doctors encouraged to enter this field. The campaign resulted in the introduction of a voluntary, three-year 'vocational' training in 1968, which was taken up with enthusiasm throughout the 70s and became mandatory in 1980. The College, meanwhile, had been awarded the Royal Charter in 1972.

Awarded the OBE in 1971, Horder edited and wrote, with five colleagues, *The Future General Practitioner: Learning and Teaching* (1972), which became a standard textbook, and formed, with a Danish doctor, the Leeuwenhorst European Working Group in 1974. This brought together 11 countries on both sides of the then Iron Curtain in an agreement about the role and training of general practitioners. He served as President of the College (1979-82) and was awarded the CBE in 1981. He officially retired in 1982, but went on to campaign for greater collaboration between the different professional groups engaged in health and social care, becoming the first Chairman of the UK Centre for the Advancement of Interprofessional Education in 1985.

'There's nothing much wrong with me piece by piece; it's what's holding me together that went wrong.'
A former patient

Main photograph: 5th July 1999, Primrose Hill, London
Inset photograph: Aged 11

ROGER BANNISTER

Sir Roger Bannister CBE, DM, FRCP
Born 1929, Harrow, England

Consultant neurologist and former British middle-distance runner, Roger Bannister shot to international fame as the first man to break the 'four-minute mile' at an athletics meeting at Iffley Road, Oxford on 6th May 1954.

Hitherto regarded as an impossible feat, dubbed 'the Everest of athletics', Bannister burst through the fabled four-minute barrier in 3 minutes 59.4 seconds, beating the Swede Gunder Hägg's world record of 4:01.4, set on 17th July 1945. A student at Oxford University, he had won the mile event in the Oxford vs. Cambridge match four times (1947-50) and come fourth in the 1500 metres at the 1952 Olympic Games in Helsinki. After the historic achievement in May, he went on to win the mile event at the Empire Games in Vancouver and the gold medal in the European 1500 metres event in 1954, which was to be his last race.

In the same year, Bannister completed his medical studies at St Mary's Hospital, London and followed his athletics success with a distinguished medical career. In 1955 he published an account of his triumph, First Four Minutes and was awarded the CBE. He went on to write several papers on the physiology of exercise and neurology and was a correspondent for The Sunday Times until 1962. Chairman of the British Sports Council from 1971 to 1974, he was knighted for services to medicine in 1975 and served as President of the International Council for Sport and Physical Recreation from 1976-83. He was Master of Pembroke College, Oxford from 1985 to 1993.

Widely regarded at the time as the man who, in one race, did more than any other athlete for years to boost British prestige on the track, Bannister will be remembered for his awesome singleness of purpose and his ground-devouring strides over the last 300 yards that completed the most memorable running time in athletics history.

Although I am remembered for the first breaking of the four minute mile 'barrier' my main life's work, and indeed my passionate interest, has been as a neurological specialist. I made fast friends through running but then as Chairman of the British Sports Council I hoped to influence people to become fitter and to give them the opportunities to do so. Fame is transitory, but the legacy I have tried to give Britain is one of better health by both my sporting and neurological work.

Main photograph: 21st March 1997
Inset photograph: Aged 2

VIVIENNE WESTWOOD

Vivienne Westwood OBE
Born Vivienne Swire, 1941, Glossop, Derbyshire

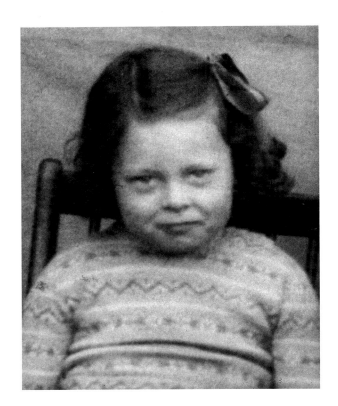

Britain's leading fashion iconoclast, Vivienne Westwood is renowned for her consistently original and controversial collections, which are steeped in historical reference and characterised by flamboyance and irony. The architect of two major fashion movements, punk rock in the 1970s and the New Romantics in the 1980s, she has sent slashed T-shirts, leather bondage gear, latex dresses, fake-fur knickers and satin codpieces marching down the catwalk for over 22 years.

Westwood trained and worked as a primary school teacher in London before meeting the rock music entrepreneur Malcolm McLaren in 1965, who became her boyfriend and artistic collaborator. They opened their first shop, Let it Rock, in the King's Road in 1971, and Westwood used it as a showcase for her emergence as a clothes designer. Initially selling zoot suits and Teddy-Boy attire, they re-named the shop Sex in 1974, and gained notoriety for their stock of leather bondage items and rubberwear for the office. In 1976 it became Seditionaries, from where Westwood and McLaren pioneered the safety-pinned bin-liners and torn stockings of punk, and fashioned the most famous punk rock band, the Sex Pistols.

In the early 80s Westwood called the shop World's End and revealed her Pirate Collection, white blouson tops and breeches that defined the New Romantic Movement, at her first catwalk show at Olympia, London in 1981. She followed it with Savage, mixing ethnic influences with historical garments topped with body paint and mud-plastered hair. A year later she showed in Paris, and further collections, including Punkature (1982) and Witches (1983), established her reputation as a highly visual and irreverent artist. In 1984 she split with McLaren and moved into couture. Her Mini Crini Collection (1985) featured crinolines and puff-ball skirts set off by her trademark platform shoes, and Portrait (1990) mixed velvet, fake-fur and city-stripe cotton with photographic prints of Old Masters on silk and fine wool.

Winner of the British Designer of the Year Award for 1990 and 1991, Westwood was awarded the OBE in 1992. She has continued to launch innovative and eccentric collections, featuring clashing tartan separates, tailored suits and Scarlet O'Hara inspired corsets and gowns, and exports to more than 30 countries worldwide.

I don't understand this desperate need to always move forward. To strive for the new is the most conformist thing you can do.

Main photograph: 26th April 1999, London
Inset photograph: Aged 3, Glossop

BERT FELSTEAD

Bertie Felstead
Born 1894, London

Veteran First World War soldier Bertie Felstead is the sole, living survivor of a Christmas Day truce between the German and British troops on the Western Front in 1915. Stationed near the village of Laventie in northern France, Felstead, a 21 year-old private in the Royal Welch Fusiliers, emerged from the icy trenches with his brothers-in-arms, against strict orders, to exchange greetings and cigarettes with the enemy in no man's land. The extraordinary meeting took place after a lone German rendition of *All Through The Night* filtered across to the British troops, who responded with *Good King Wenceslas*, after which both sides clambered over their respective parapets, having spent months trying to kill each other, and shook hands in a poignant moment in world history.

Educated in Cheshunt, Felstead worked in a nursery garden before volunteering for service in early 1915. He joined the Royal Welch Fusiliers in London and began training in Llandudno and on Salisbury Plain, before being sent to France. Following the 1915 truce, he was wounded in the Battle of the Somme in July 1916 and sent to Ireland to recover, after which he volunteered for service overseas and was dispatched to the Greek island of Salonika. He returned to England after contracting malaria, married his sweetheart Alice in 1918, and went back to France for the final stretch of the war. Demobbed in 1919, he settled in Ruislip before moving to Gloucester in 1939, and worked for the Air Ministry for the next 36 years. He was a commissionaire for the General Electric Company for 12 years, and became the evening caretaker for a local college until his retirement in 1974, on his 80th birthday.

Felstead was awarded the Queen's Coronation Medal in 1953 and was appointed to the Légion d'Honneur in 1998. At 104 years of age, he is a father of three, grandfather of five, great-grandfather of 13 and great-great-grandfather of one.

Of course we realised we were in the most extraordinary position, wishing each other Happy Christmas one day, and shooting each other the next, but we were so pleased to be able to forget the war and shake hands.

Main photograph: 11th February 1997, Gloucestershire
Inset photograph: Aged 21, Cheshunt, Hertfordshire, 1915

RANULPH FIENNES

Sir Ranulph Twisleton-Wykeham-Fiennes OBE
Born 1944, Windsor

Dubbed 'the world's greatest living explorer' by the *Guinness Book of Records*, Sir Ranulph Fiennes has led ten major expeditions across the Arctic and Antarctic between 1969 and 1994. A veteran soldier turned polar explorer, his record-breaking treks have pushed the boundaries of human endurance and greatly extended our knowledge of the physical world.

Brought up in South Africa but educated at Eton, Fiennes served as a Lieutenant in the Royal Scots Greys before joining the Special Air Service (SAS) in 1966, aged 22. In 1968 he was seconded to the Sultan's Armed Forces in Oman and spent two years fighting communist insurgents, for which he was awarded the Sultan's medal for bravery. In 1969 he led his first expedition, journeying up the White Nile by hovercraft and surveying a Norwegian glacier, and followed that by canoeing across British Columbia. He left the army, and in 1979, after six years of intensive planning, embarked on the gruelling four-year Trans Globe Expedition, the first surface journey around the world's polar axis.

In 1986, in an attempt to reach the North Pole, Fiennes broke the world record by 300 miles for the furthest unsupported expedition, for which he received the Polar Medal in 1987. In 1990 he became co-leader of the Ubar Expedition, a mission to find the lost city of Ubar in the Arabian desert, during which he discovered Ptolemy's long-lost Atlantis of the Sands in 1991. The Pentland South Pole Expedition, however, proved to be his greatest triumph. He and Dr. Michael Stroud achieved the first totally self-supported sledge journey across the Antarctic Continent, the longest unsupported polar journey in history, covering the 2,170 km (1,350 miles) from Gould Bay to the Ross ice shelf in Antarctica in 94 days between 9 November 1992 and 16th January 1993.

By 1993 his expeditions had raised more than £6 million for charity, and Fiennes was awarded the OBE for 'human endeavour and charitable services'. In 1995, in recognition of his achievements in Polar exploration, he was awarded a second clasp to the Polar Medal, becoming the only explorer to have earned a double clasp, acknowledging both Arctic and Antarctic achievements. He has published numerous books, including his autobiography *Living Dangerously* (1987, 1994) and *Mind Over Matter* (1997).

Whatever you can do, or dream you can ...begin it.
A tribute to Goethe from a translation of *Faust* by J.Anster (1835)

RICHARD DOLL

Sir Richard Doll CH, OBE, DM, MD, DSc., FRCP, FRS
Born 1912, Hampton

Richard Doll is the eminent epidemiologist who, in collaboration with the late statistician Austin Bradford Hill, provided the first statistical proof of the link between cancer and smoking in 1950, and has since established an international reputation as a leading authority in the field of cancer research.

Doll graduated from St Thomas's Hospital Medical School in London in 1937, before serving as a medical officer in France and the Middle East during World War Two. He became a member of the Medical Research Council's Statistical Research Unit in 1948 and joined forces with Hill to begin studying the cause of the rapid increase in mortality attributed to lung cancer. They focused their attention on the agents that affected the quality of the air, such as car exhaust fumes, the materials used for tarring roads and cigarette smoke, and were able to provide conclusive evidence, published in the *British Medical Journal* in 1950, that cigarette smoke was the principal cause of the disease.

Doll was awarded the OBE in 1956, appointed Director of the Statistical Research Unit in 1961, and received the United Nations Award for Cancer Research in 1962. During the subsequent three decades he was a key figure in the establishment of clinical trials and epidemiological studies which revealed the potentially harmful effects of asbestos, ionising radiation and oral contraceptives, and further concluded that many cancers are caused by diet. Director of the Imperial Cancer Research Fund's Cancer Epidemiology and Clinical Trials Unit (1978-83, 1987-89), he has won numerous awards for his pioneering work, including the British Medical Association Gold Medal in 1983 and Royal Society Royal Medal in 1986.

Doll retired in 1989 but continued to work as an honorary member of the Clinical Trial Service Unit and Epidemiological Studies Unit at Oxford University, and began studying the possible effects of electro-magnetic fields on childhood cancers. He was awarded the Royal Society of Medicine Gold Medal in 1997 and the British Thoracic Society Medal in 1998. His research into the causes of cancer has had a radical impact on the medical profession's understanding and treatment of the disease, and has formed the basis of a series of government health campaigns aimed at raising public awareness of the damaging risk to health caused by cigarettes.

Years may wrinkle the skin, but to give up enthusiasm wrinkles the soul.
From *Youth*, by Samuel Ullman (1840-1924)

Main photograph: 30th June 1998, Oxford
Inset photograph: Aged 18, before giving up smoking

VIRGINIA WADE

Virginia Wade OBE
Born 1945, Bournemouth

One of the finest figures of British tennis, Virginia Wade became a household name in 1977 when she won the Ladies Singles Championship at Wimbledon. A Federation Cup player for Great Britain for 18 years, and participant in the Wightman Cup for 21 years, she has competed in a record 25 consecutive Wimbledon championships.

Wade grew up in Durban, South Africa, and returned to England when she was 15. She made her debut at Wimbledon in 1962, aged just 16, and turned professional in 1968 after winning the first open tennis tournament held in Bournemouth. A skilful player, with one of the most powerful serves on the circuit, Wade consistently maintained a top ten ranking from 1967-79, confirming her world-class status with Grand Slam singles honours in the US Open Championships in 1968, the Italian Open in 1971 and the Australian Open in 1972. She teamed up with Margaret Court in the women's doubles and won the US, French and Australian Championships in 1973, followed by a second US victory in 1975.

Her finest hour came in 1977, however, when, aged 32, in her 16th Wimbledon championship, in the year of the Queen's Silver Jubilee and the 100th anniversary of Wimbledon, she beat defending champion Chris Evert 6-2,4-6,6-1 in the semi-finals and toppled Betty Stover 4-6,6-3,6-1 in a rousing final, to seize the trophy. Such was the intensity of patriotism in the air that the oldest first-time winner of Wimbledon was treated to the entire Centre Court crowd's jubilant rendition of *For She's A Jolly Good Fellow*.

Wade continued to play on tour for eight years following her Wimbledon victory, and officially retired in December 1985. Awarded the OBE a year later, she has competed in the 35-and-over women's doubles at Wimbledon every year since the event began in 1990, winning the title five times with Wendy Turnbull. Credited with significantly boosting the image of British tennis, Wade became the first woman to be elected to the Wimbledon Championships Committee in 1983, and is a respected commentator on the sport in Britain and abroad.

I'm in the final for the first time.
The Queen is watching. Everybody is watching.
I'm going to win this thing if I have to kill myself to do it.
I am going home today with something I have dreamed about from the moment
I knew it existed. And I'm going to send everybody else home with a piece of it...
We are all co-producers of this event, every last one of us.
And when I've won this title I will look in the eyes of every single face and say thank you.
Thank you for believing in me.
Thank you for caring.
Thank you for waiting....
July 1977, Wimbledon

ISAIAH BERLIN

Sir Isaiah Berlin OM, CBE
Born 1909, Riga, Latvia

Isaiah Berlin is regarded as one of the most influential thinkers of the 20th century. Dubbed 'the wisest man in Britain', his writings on philosophy, political theory and the history of ideas encapsulate the principal movements of the modern age and are required reading for all students of philosophy.

The son of a Jewish timber-merchant, Berlin witnessed the Russian Revolution at the age of eight, before his family fled to England in 1921. He won a scholarship to Oxford, studying philosophy and classics, and was the first Jew ever elected to All Souls. He spent the 30s teaching philosophy, and published a celebrated study of Karl Marx in 1939. During the war he was sent by the Ministry of Information to Washington, where his confidential reports on US opinion caught Winston Churchill's attention, and he later became a key figure in the intellectual movement against communism during the Cold War.

In 1945 he was seconded to the British Embassy in Moscow, and had an encounter with the persecuted poet Anna Akhmatova which had a profound effect on his life. He returned to England with an intense loathing of tyranny and an increased interest in the history of ideas, to which he dedicated the rest of his career. In 1953 he published his famous essay on Tolstoy, *The Hedgehog and the Fox*, in which he created a modern metaphor from the Greek poet Archilochus' line, 'The fox knows many things – the hedgehog one big thing'. In 1957 he became Chichele Professor of Social and Political Theory and in 1958 published his seminal essay, *Two Concepts of Liberty*, in which he advanced a crucial distinction between 'positive' and 'negative' liberty, the freedom of self-realisation and the freedom from restraints placed upon us.

A Russian, Jew and Englishman, Berlin was an exponent of pluralism, a view reflected in the 1998 anthology of his essays, *The Proper Study of Mankind*, which also confirm his moral position that mutual tolerance is the greater part of liberty and fanaticism the source of the greatest evils. The first President of Wolfson College, Oxford, Berlin was knighted in 1957 and made a member of the Order of Merit in 1971. He died on 6th November 1997, aged 88.

These values are the basis of what I believe: that decent respect for others and the toleration of dissent are better than pride and a sense of national mission; that liberty may be incompatible with, and better than, too much efficiency; that pluralism and untidiness are, to those who value freedom, better than the rigorous imposition of all-embracing systems, no matter how rational or disinterested, or than the rule of majorities against which there is no appeal. All this is deeply and uniquely English, and I freely admit that I am steeped in it, and believe in it, and cannot breathe freely save in a society where these values are for the most part taken for granted. 'Out of the crooked timber of humanity', said Immanuel Kant, 'no straight thing was ever made.'
The Three Strands of My Life, from *Personal Impressions* (2nd Edition,1998)

Main photograph: 18th November 1996, The Albany, Piccadilly, London
Inset photograph: Aged 8, Petrograd, Russia

RICHARD HAMILTON

Richard Hamilton
Born 1922, London

The pioneer of Pop Art, Richard Hamilton has been a seminal figure in British art for more than forty years. His work, which merges fine art with the techniques and forms of many non-fine-art media such as movement and sound, has sought to trace the human experience in an ever-changing social and political landscape.

Hamilton studied painting at the Royal Academy Schools in 1937 before serving as a draughtsman during World War Two. After national service he studied at the Slade School of Art, and held his first solo exhibition in 1950. He began teaching at the Central School for Arts and Crafts in 1952 and, fascinated by the new, high-tech consumer goods flooding into Britain, founded the Independent Group at the ICA, a forum for artists and intellectuals to discuss aspects of popular culture.

In 1955 Hamilton exhibited paintings at the Hanover Gallery in London and designed the *Man, Machine and Motion* exhibition at the ICA. He rose to prominence a year later with a series of groundbreaking exhibitions, notably *This is Tomorrow* at the Whitechapel Art Gallery, which introduced the concept of pop art with the celebrated collage picture *Just What is It That Makes Today's Homes so Different, so Appealing?* The work fused painting with printed imagery, such as photographs and advertisements, to create an ironic commentary on contemporary culture and won instant international acclaim.

Politics and social change remain central themes in Hamilton's art, and his best known works include *Hommage à Chrysler Corp* (1952), *Study of Hugh Gaitskell as a Famous Monster of Film Land* (1964) and his reconstruction of Marcel Duchamp's *Le Grand Verre* (1965). In 1979 his first retrospective exhibition was held at the Tate Gallery, and in 1993 he shared the Leone D'Oro prize for Best Artist with Antoni Tapies at the Venice Biennale, exhibiting *The Citizen* (1981-83), a work based on the 1980 BBC TV film about IRA prisoners in the Maze.

Whilst Pop Art remains the principal aspect of Hamilton's legacy, his work as a painter, teacher, curator and spokesman for artists has established him as a key figure in Britain's expanding cultural relationship with the wider world.

Pop Art is:
Popular (designed for a mass audience)
Transient (short-term solution)
Expendable (easily forgotten)
Low cost
Mass produced
Young (aimed at youth)
Witty
Sexy
Gimmicky
Glamorous
Big business
Hamilton, 1957

Main photograph: 26th November 1998, Oxford
Inset photograph: Aged 12

HENRY COOPER

Henry Cooper OBE
Born 1934, Bellingham, Kent

Henry Cooper was the British heavyweight champion boxer who guaranteed his place in history by being the first Briton to knock down the world champion Muhammed Ali. Canonised, ironically, for a fight he actually lost, 'Our Enry' floored Ali in the fourth round of the Cooper-Clay non-title fight of 1963, before suffering so severe a bout of blows to his face that the fight was curtailed in the fifth round.

Cooper began boxing in his teens, training with his twin brother George, also a talented sportsman, and was soon tipped as an outstanding prospect. His rise to prominence began when he won the Amateur Boxing Association light-heavyweight championship in 1952 and again in 1953, after which he turned professional. He shot to fame in 1959 when he beat Brian London to win the British and Commonwealth professional heavyweight championship, a title which he held for a record ten years and five months until 1970, defending the crown eight times and becoming the first man ever to win three Lonsdale belts. In spite of his tendency to cut easily, his powerful left hook, known as 'Enry's 'Ammer', ensured his dominance in the ring and added three European heavyweight titles, from 1964-70, to his list of victories. In 1966 he confronted Ali for the second time with the World Title at stake, but was forced to retire, this time in the sixth round, again due to bad cuts.

Twice voted by the BBC as Sports Personality of the Year, Cooper was awarded the OBE in 1969 and retired in 1971, following the loss of his British heavyweight title in a disputed contest against Joe Bugner. A keen golfer, he has since devoted much of his time to playing in Pro-Am and Celebrity-Am golf tournaments for a number of charities, notably the Variety Club of Great Britain Golfing Society, of which he is chairman.

'Cooper shook me up. He hit me harder than I've ever been hit before. I've been on the floor before, but not hurt so much. I underestimated him, he's a real fighter.'
Muhammed Ali, after the 1963 fight

Main photograph: 7th October 1998, Tonbridge, Kent
Inset photograph: Aged 5

TOM STOPPARD

Sir Tom Stoppard CBE
Born Thomas Straussler, 1937, Zlin, Czechoslovakia

Tom Stoppard is one of the most successful writers in modern, British theatre, whose body of work is characterised by a comic combination of grand, philosophical themes, elaborate structures and stylish, verbal gymnastics.

Arriving in England in 1946, having spent his early childhood in India, Stoppard was educated in Yorkshire, and began his writing career as a journalist with local papers in Bristol. In 1960 he penned his first play, A Walk on Water, later renamed Enter a Free Man, and made his radio debut with The Dissolution of Dominic Boot, broadcast by the BBC in 1964.

He rose to prominence with his stage play Rosencrantz and Guildenstern are Dead, an existentialist comedy built around the two 'attendant lords' in Shakespeare's Hamlet, which premiered at the Edinburgh Festival before playing at the National Theatre in London in 1967, winning the Evening Standard Award for Best Play. Stoppard followed it with a series of acclaimed plays throughout the 70s, notably Jumpers in 1972, a farcical satire of logical positivism, and Travesties in 1974, which presented the bizarre trio of James Joyce, Lenin and the Dadaist painter Tristan Tzara, collaborating on an amateur production of Oscar Wilde's The Importance of Being Ernest. In 1977 he produced Every Good Boy Deserves Favour for the London stage and Professional Foul for BBC Television, and was awarded the CBE a year later. He went on to write the stage plays Night and Day (1978), The Real Thing (1982) and an adaptation of Vaclav Havel's Large Desolato (1986), among others.

In the 80s Stoppard diversified into writing for feature films and produced screenplays for adaptations of Graham Greene's The Human Factor (1980), J.G. Ballard's Empire of the Sun (1987) and John Le Carre's The Russia House (1990). In 1990 he scripted and directed the film version of Rosencrantz and Guildenstern are Dead, which won the Grand Prize at the Venice Film Festival, and produced the stage plays Arcadia (1993) and Indian Ink (1995). The Invention of Love premiered at the National Theatre in 1997, winning the Evening Standard Drama Award for Best Play, and in the same year, Stoppard became the first British playwright to be knighted since Terence Rattigan.

In 1999, he shared the Oscar for Best Original Screenplay and a Golden Globe Award with fellow writer Marc Norman for the hugely successful film Shakespeare in Love.

'It's wanting to know that makes us matter. Otherwise, we're going out the way we came in.'
Hannah Jarvis in Act II, Scene VII of Stoppard's *Arcadia*, 1993

NORMAN HEATLEY

Dr. Norman Heatley DM (Hon) Oxon
Born 1911, Woodbridge, Suffolk

Biochemist Norman Heatley was a crucial figure in the development of the antibiotic penicillin, devising an essential method of purification and constructing an efficient, if unconventional, system of producing sufficient quantities to perform the first clinical trials.

After obtaining his Ph.D from Cambridge University in 1936, Heatley was employed as a bacteriologist to work with chemist Ernst Chain in pathologist Howard Florey's team at the William Dunn School of Pathology in Oxford in 1939. The team already had a sample of the mould discovered by Alexander Fleming in 1928 but were having difficulty extracting the active ingredient from the liquid produced by the mould. The chemical properties were unstable – just one part in two million was penicillin – and when the solvents used to extract the penicillin from the impurity were evaporated, much of the penicillin was lost. Heatley's first contribution was the invention of the 'cylinder plate assay method', a means by which the strength of the purified extracts could be determined. He then suggested the ingenious chemical trick of transferring the penicillin back into water by changing the acidity.

Having extracted the raw penicillin, the team set about cultivating sufficient quantities to begin tests on animals. Equipment was low due to rationing but Heatley managed to construct an elaborate Heath-Robinson style-production line, adapting pie dishes, flasks, biscuit tins and bedpans into suitable containers. In May 1940 eight mice were injected with a fatal dose of the disease germ streptococci. Four mice were set aside as 'controls', the other four were treated with penicillin. Within hours, the 'controls' were dead, but those treated were alive and apparently well, providing the first evidence of the life-saving properties of the drug.

Florey realised that penicillin could have an effect on the outcome of the war, and made plans to produce enough of it for the first clinical trials. Heatley had special rectangular ceramic culture vessels manufactured, and invented a natty gadget to better facilitate the harvesting of the liquid. In 1941 six patients at Oxford's Radcliffe Infirmary were successfully treated with the drug and the results, published in *The Lancet* that August, confirmed penicillin as a safe and potent cure for bacterial infections. Large-scale manufacture ensured that by 1944 it was available to every allied casualty who could benefit from it.

In 1990, 50 years after his crucial work, Heatley was awarded an honorary Doctorate of Medicine from Oxford University, one of only two non-medically qualified people to receive such an award in the University's 800-year history.

After supper with some friends, I returned to the lab, and met the Professor to give a final dose of penicillin to two of the mice. The 'controls' were looking very sick, but the treated mice seemed very well. I stayed at the lab, until 3.45am by which time all 4 control animals were dead. It really looks as if penicillin may be of practical importance....
Extract from Heatley's diary, 25th May 1940.

Main photograph: 26th November 1998, Old Marston, Oxford
Inset photograph: Aged 9

ROY JENKINS

The Rt. Hon. Lord Jenkins of Hillhead OM
Born 1920, Monmouthshire, Wales

Liberal peer, former Labour Home Secretary and co-founder of the Social Democrat Party, Roy Jenkins is the elder statesman of the British political centre. The youngest MP at the time of his election to the House of Commons in 1948, he is a distinguished writer and award-winning political biographer.

The son of a Labour MP, Jenkins was educated at Oxford University before serving in the Army and working at Bletchley Park during World War Two. Elected MP for Central Southwark in 1948, aged 27, he served as a parliamentary private secretary under Clement Attlee at 28, and in 1950, became MP for Stetchford, Birmingham. Throughout the 50s he spearheaded a campaign to liberalise the obscenity laws to strengthen the position of authors and publishers against prosecution, which culminated in the introduction of the controversial Obscene Publications Bill in 1958. In 1965 he was appointed Home Secretary in Harold Wilson's cabinet, before moving to the Treasury as Chancellor of the Exchequer in 1967. Following Labour's defeat in 1970 he became deputy leader, but resigned in 1972 in a dispute with Wilson over British entry into the European Community. When Labour returned to power in 1974 he resumed his position as Home Secretary, resigning from Parliament in 1976 after unsuccessfully standing for the leadership against James Callaghan.

A year later Jenkins was appointed President of the European Commission, where he oversaw the launch of the European Monetary System. In March 1981 he and MPs Shirley Williams, David Owen and William Rodgers broke with Labour to launch the centrist Social Democratic Party (SDP) which merged with the Liberals in 1988. In 1982 he was elected MP for Glasgow (Hillhead), becoming the first leader of the SDP before relinquishing the post to Owen the following year.

Jenkins retired from Parliament in 1987 and was created a Life Peer, taking his seat in the Lords with the Liberal Democrats. He was awarded the Order of Merit in 1992, and in 1998 he was appointed by Tony Blair to head the Commission on Electoral Reform, which aimed to radically transform our democracy.

The likelihood before the start of most adventures is that of failure. The experimental plane may well finish up a few fields from the end of the run-way. If this is so, the voluntary occupants will have only inflicted bruises or worse upon themselves. But the reverse could occur and the experimental plane soar into the sky.
Jenkins's speech to the Parliamentary Press Gallery, 9th June 1980

IRIS MURDOCH

Dame Iris Murdoch
Born 1919, Dublin, Ireland

Distinguished novelist, philosopher and intellectual, Dame Iris Murdoch was one of the most intriguing and influential British writers of the post-war period. Her large body of work included 26 novels, plays and poetry and often combined philosophical speculation within comical tales of tangled human relationships.

After graduating from Oxford University in 1942, Murdoch worked for the Treasury, before joining the United Nations Rehabilitation and Relief Association in 1944, working with refugees in Europe. She went on to study philosophy at Newnham College, Cambridge and returned to Oxford in 1948 as tutor of philosophy at St. Anne's College. She published her first academic book, *Sartre, Romantic Rationalist*, in 1953, followed a year later by her first novel, Under The Net, the story of an anarchic caper in London and Paris, heavily influenced by Sartre and Beckett.

The novels The Sandcastle and The Bell were published in 1957 and 1958 respectively, and in 1961 Murdoch gained international recognition for her black comedy, A Severed Head. She published numerous best-selling novels throughout the 60s and 70s, including *The Italian Girl* (1964), *A Fairly Honourable Defeat* (1970), *The Sacred and Profane Love Machine* (1974), *The Sovereignty of Good* (1970) and *The Fire and the Sun* (1977). She also dramatised her novel *A Severed Head* (1963) and wrote the plays *Servants and The Snow* (1970) and *The Two Arrows* (1972), before being awarded the CBE in 1976.

Critically acclaimed for the originality, complexity, humour and humanity of her fiction, Murdoch was shortlisted for the Booker Prize six times, finally triumphing in 1978 with The Sea, The Sea, a compelling tale of obsessional love, thought by many to be her finest novel. A volume of poetry, The Year of the Birds, followed, as well as many other novels throughout the Eighties, such as *The Good Apprentice* (1985). Awarded a DBE in 1987, her final philosophical text, Metaphysics as a Guide to Morals, was published in 1992, followed by her last novel, *Jackson's Dilemma* in 1995. Dame Iris Murdoch was diagnosed with Alzheimer's Disease in 1995 and died in February 1999.

People are very secretive and people, for many purposes, want to appear ordinary. They conceal even quite simple aspects of their lives and desires. Any character is interesting and has extremes. People have extremes, fears and passions they perhaps don't admit to. It is the novelist's privelege to be able to see just how odd everybody is.

1986

TOM DENNING

The Rt. Hon. Lord Denning of Whitchurch OM. DL
Born Alfred Thompson Denning. 1899. Hampshire

Lord Denning was Britain's most celebrated, controversial and influential judge this century. Heralded as 'the people's judge', his willingness to override precedent to do what he saw as justice, and his crusade to defend the rights of the individual against the might of government and commerce, has left an unprecedented mark on English law.

Denning was Educated at Oxford University and called to the Bar in 1923. He became a KC in 1938 and a judge of the High Court of Justice in 1944 at the age of 45, the youngest on the bench. Five years later he was appointed to the Court of Appeal and thereafter to the House of Lords. He served as Master of the Rolls from 1962-82.

He became a household name in 1963 when he headed the inquiry into the Profumo affair. His report on the War Secretary's affair with a prostitute became a key legal document of the 60s and an instant best-seller. Among many celebrated judgements, Denning eased divorce procedures, championing the deserted wife and giving her an equity in the family home, and was the first to create property rights for cohabitees. He steadfastly overturned decisions of the war pensions tribunal refusing applications for pensions, and allowed Freddie Laker to compete against British Airways, paving the way for cheap air travel.

A firm believer that justice should meet the circumstances of each case, Denning's tendency towards judicial law-making of his own occasionally led to complaints of subjectivity and inconsistency, and he was invariably unpredictable. But his defence of individual rights, expressed in his lucid prose, contributed to his immense popularity and the public benches of his court were routinely crowded with law students and tourists, eager to witness the great man in action.

His retirement in 1982, after a 38-year judicial career, was sparked by controversy surrounding the third volume of his legal reminiscences, *What Next In The Law?*, in which he made some recommendations about jury selection which exposed him to the charge of racism. This, and some other illiberal comments made in his declining years, took some of the shine off his reputation. But Denning, uncompromising and inspirational, will be remembered for his profound passion for justice and independence of mind.

Lord Denning died on 5th March 1999, six weeks after his hundreth birthday.

What is the argument on the other side? Only this, that no case has been found in which it has been done before. That argument does not appeal to me in the least. If we never do anything which has not been done before, we shall never get anywhere. The law will stand still whilst the rest of the world goes on; and that will be bad for both.
Denning L J in *Packer v Packer*, 1954. P15 at 22

Main photograph: 15th August 1997, Whitchurch, Hampshire
Inset photograph: Aged 7

ANTHONY CARO

Sir Anthony Caro CBE
Born 1924, London

Feted as Britain's greatest living sculptor, Anthony Caro has established an international reputation for his innovative and prodigious output during the last 50 years. The pre-eminent exponent of constructed sculpture, he made his name in the early 1960s with dramatic, abstract steel sculptures, and collections of his work now feature in 98 museums worldwide.

Caro studied engineering at Cambridge University before serving with the Fleet Air Arm during World War Two. He took his first art course at Regent Street Polytechnic in 1946 and enrolled at the Royal Academy Schools in London a year later. In 1951, frustrated by what he believed to be the constraints of formal academic training, he became a part-time assistant to Henry Moore, whose monumental abstract sculptures had long fascinated him.

Throughout the 50s he concentrated on massive, figurative bronzes, such as *Man Taking Off His Shirt*, which was exhibited in Milan in 1956, but gained little critical recognition. A meeting in 1959 with the American avant-garde artist David Smith, however, whose abstract iron and steel work had generated considerable notoriety, provided the turning point in his career. He took a course in welding, completed his first steel work, *24 Hours*, and won the Paris Biennale Prize for sculpture.

Caro developed a new abstract style characterised by large pieces of iron and steel rods, pipes and I-beams, welded together and painted in bold primary colours, displayed without the customary plinth or base, which met with great acclaim. In 1966 he won the David E. Bright Prize at the Venice Biennale for a body of work consisting of *Midday* (1960), *Early One Morning* (1962), and *Titan* (1964); and in the 1970s, working with large pieces of rusted and varnished factory steel, and 'found' scraps of weathered steel, he produced the celebrated 'Emma' sculptures, notably *Emma Dipper* (1977), at the Emma Lake Artists Workshop in Canada.

Knighted in 1987, Caro won the Henry Moore Grand Prize in 1991, and three years later, had the largest retrospective exhibition of his work mounted at the Museum of Contemporary Art in Tokyo. In collaboration with architect Norman Foster, he won the 1996 Millennium Bridge Design commission for a new footbridge across the Thames, and in 1999, premiered a monumental, 25-unit work at the Venice Biennale, called *The Last Judgement*, comprising individual, wood-based sculptures such as *Jacob's Ladder*, *Gate of Heaven* and *Tribunal*.

Sculpture, for me, is something outside of which you are. It's not something you can get inside; it's not architecture or environment. I put this limit on sculpture and I think by so doing, I gain more freedom, not less. Every generation allows for sculpture or painting a little different theatre of operations than before. And all new art at the time it is made is about going as close to the edge as possible, but without losing one's foothold.

HELEN BAMBER

Helen Bamber OBE, DU (Essex)
Born 1925, London

Human rights campaigner Helen Bamber is the founder of the Medical Foundation for the Care of Victims of Torture. A witness to the unspeakable horrors of genocide in the latter half of the century, from Belsen to Bosnia, she has dedicated her life to the rehabilitation of survivors of despotic regimes worldwide, and lobbied vociferously against state-sponsored cruelty.

The daughter of Jews of Polish extraction, living in Britain, Bamber grew up under the veil of the fascist threat. In 1945, aged 20, she volunteered for service with the Jewish Relief Unit and travelled to Germany to care for survivors of the Belsen concentration camp. She dispensed food and clothing, and rapidly became aware of the need for emotional as well as practical support for the traumatised victims. On her return to London in 1947 she was appointed to the Committee for the Care of Children from Concentration Camps and, in collaboration with the Anna Freud Clinic, cared for 720 orphans from Auschwitz.

Working for a variety of hospitals and health organisations throughout the 50s, Bamber was influenced by the findings of Dr. Maurice Pappworth, a physician who exposed the unethical practice of doctors conducting medical experiments on their patients, and she joined Amnesty International in 1961. Horrifed by the stories of sophisticated, institutionalised torture that had begun to emerge from a number of South American countries during the 1970s, she set up Amnesty's first British medical team in 1975, to research and document evidence of torture.

Operating out of a basement garage at Amnesty's London HQ, Bamber soon realised the need for a support centre to treat victims seeking refuge in Britain. In 1985 she left Amnesty to set up the Medical Foundation for the Care of Victims of Torture at the former National Temperance Hospital in Hampstead, north London. Now based in Kentish Town, her charitable organisation has provided medical treatment, practical assistance, counselling and psychotherapy to more than 16,500 survivors of torture, and their families, in the UK. Awarded the OBE in 1997, Bamber has helped to establish similar aid projects around the world, and campaigned for an improved legislative framework for the treatment of asylum seekers and refugees.

Belsen had a very strange smell. It wasn't an unpleasant smell, it was a rather sweet smell, like crushed geraniums, and I often smell those geraniums on my patio. It's about not denying: it's about remembering, never forgetting, the need to constantly bear witness.

HARRISON BIRTWISTLE

Sir Harrison Birtwistle
Born 1934, Accrington, Lancashire

Harrison Birtwistle is one of the most innovative and challenging composers of the 20th century. Influenced by Stravinsky and the Renaissance masters, and inspired by contemporary art and classic mythology, he is an avant-garde artist celebrated for his creation of a complex, sculptural and intensely expressive musical language.

Passionate about music from childhood, Birtwistle composed his first wind quartet aged 13, and won a scholarship to study composition at the Royal Manchester College of Music in 1952. Teaming up with contemporaries Peter Maxwell Davies, Alexander Goehr and John Ogden, he formed the New Music Manchester Group for the performance of contemporary music. After studying the clarinet at the Royal Academy of Music, he achieved his first critical successes in 1965 with the instrumental *Tragoedia* and the vocal instrumental *Ring A Dumb Carillon*. His first opera, *Punch and Judy*, was premiered at the Aldeburgh festival in 1968, and its dramatic score, as with those of his 1969 *Down by the Greenwood Side* and *The Triumph of Time* (1972), was redolent of the multilayering, repetition and explosive movement which were to become his trademark.

The decade from 1973 to 1984 was dominated by the composition of Birtwistle's biggest opera, the lyric tragedy *The Mask of Orpheus*, which was premiered by the English National Opera in 1986 and for which he received the Grawemeyer Award. He also wrote a series of acclaimed ensemble scores, such as *Silbury Air* (1977), *Secret Theatre* (1984) and the major orchestral work *Earth Dances* (1986), considered his most spectacular piece. Knighted in 1988, he gained critical acclaim for his operas *Gawain* (1991) and *The Second Mrs Kong* (1994). His score *Panic*, written for saxophone, drum and orchestra, was premiered at the 1995 BBC Proms and his orchestral work, *Exody*, was premiered by the Chicago Symphony Orchestra in 1998.

Director of Composition at London's Royal College of Music, Birtwistle is Henry Purcell Professor of Composition at King's College, London, and Composer in Residence with the London Philharmonic Orchestra.

When from your sleepy mind the day's burden
Falls like a bushel sack on a barn floor.
Be prepared for music, for natural mirages
And for a night's incomparable parade of colour...
From *Secret Theatre*, by Robert Graves, 1970

Main photograph: 15th November 1998, Mere, Wiltshire
Inset photograph: Aged 15

PETER HALL

Sir Peter Hall CBE
Born 1930, Bury St Edmunds

Charismatic champion of the arts, Peter Hall is one of the world's most innovative and prolific arts directors. Widely revered as the principal architect of modern British theatre, he has premiered works by some of the century's most celebrated dramatists, such as Samuel Beckett and Harold Pinter, and directed numerous operas, television dramas and films.

After graduating from Cambridge University, Hall worked in repertory theatre before becoming assistant director of the London Arts Theatre. He became director in 1955 and, aged just 24, took a risk on the prevailing mood and premiered the English language version of Beckett's *Waiting For Godot*. It was a smash hit and firmly established him as Britain's most talented young director. After directing his first Shakespeare play at Stratford Memorial Theatre in 1956 he formed his own company, The International Playwrights' Theatre, in 1957.

A year later he founded the celebrated Royal Shakespeare Company and directed 18 plays during his decade-long tenure with them, notably setting many of the classics within an identifiable social context. He also premiered several plays by Pinter, including *The Homecoming* in 1965. In 1973 he succeeded Laurence Olivier as Director of the Royal National Theatre (RNT) and oversaw acclaimed productions such as *No Man's Land* (1975), *Amadeus* (1979) and *The Oresteia* (1981).

Knighted in 1977, Hall remained at the helm of the RNT for 15 years and won numerous Tony Awards before launching the Peter Hall Company in 1988. Distinguished productions included *Orpheus Descending* with Vanessa Redgrave and *The Merchant of Venice* with Dustin Hoffman. He returned to the RSC in 1992 to direct *All's Well That Ends Well* and the world premiere of Peter Shaffer's *The Gift of the Gorgon*, and in 1998 he transferred his Peter Hall Company to the Piccadilly Theatre.

Artistic Director at Glyndebourne Festival Opera from 1984 to 1990, he has directed more than 40 operas worldwide, as well as films for television and cinema. Renowned for his long and vigorous battle to increase subsidy for the arts, and disillusioned by what he believes to be a complacency in successive British governments' attitude to the theatre, Hall is now working much more in America.

As the political and economic challenge to theatre grows more threatening, its power and uniqueness as a living place for the exercise of the imagination correspondingly increases. Everyday the theatre becomes harder to save. And every day society needs it more desperately.

ARTHUR C. CLARKE

Sir Arthur C. Clarke CBE
Born 1917, Minehead, Somerset

Arthur C. Clarke is one of the world's greatest science fiction writers, most famous for the classic *2001: A Space Odyssey* and his uncannily accurate predictions of the future, which have encompassed satellite communications, lap-top computers, videophones and artificial intelligence.

Clarke was fascinated by technology and astronomy from an early age. In his teens he constructed refractor telescopes using magic lantern lenses and magnifying glasses, and endlessly tinkered with radio. He worked as a radar instructor during World War Two and was the first person to suggest that a satellite orbiting at a specific altitude over the equator, now referred to as the 'Clarke Orbit', would be 'geo-stationary' and therefore ideal for a communications relay. He published his findings in the now celebrated 'Extra-Terrestrial Relays' report in *Wireless World* in 1945 and earned himself the nickname of the 'Godfather of the Communications Satellite'.

He studied physics and mathematics at Kings College, London and joined the Institution of Electrical Engineers in 1949. Obsessed with the idea of space exploration and man's position in the hierarchy of the universe, he wrote his first factual book, *Interplanetary Flight* (1950) and his first science fiction novel, *Prelude to Space* (1951), both based on solid scientific principles, and won plaudits for the authenticity of his narrative. He left his job to write full-time, and then emigrated to Sri Lanka in 1956, from where he has penned over 80 fiction and non-fiction works such as *The Nine Billion Names of God* (1967) and *The Fountains of Paradise* (1979), winning every major science fiction award.

He commentated on the Apollo missions for CBS TV, and in 1968 was rocketed to international fame with the release of the film adaptation of *2001: A Space Odyssey*, which earned him and director Stanley Kubrick an Oscar nomination. The story foresaw space stations and talking computers, and introduced a new breed of non-menacing alien which influenced a generation of writers and directors. A recipient of the Lindbergh Award in 1987, Clarke was knighted in 1998 and remains an influential voice in scientific circles.

Our galaxy is now in the brief springtime of its life – a springtime made glorious by such brilliant blue-white stars as Vega and Sirius. Not until all these have flamed through their incandescent youth, in a few fleeting billions of years, will the real history of the universe begin. It will be a history illuminated by the reds and infra-reds of dully glowing stars, visible only to whatever strange beings have adapted to their light. Before them will lie not the billions of years in which we measure eras of geology, but years to be counted literally in trillions. They will have time enough, in those endless aeons, to attempt all things, and to gather all knowledge. They will not be like gods, because no gods imagined by our minds have ever possessed the powers they will command. But for all that, they may envy us, basking in the bright afterglow of Creation: for we knew the Universe when it was young.

Main photograph: 13th October 1998, London via satellite link-up from Colombo, Sri Lanka
Inset photograph: Aged 18, at Bishops Lydeard, Somerset.

CHRISTOPHER COCKERELL

Sir Christopher Cockerell CBE, FRS
Born 1910, Cambridge

Pioneering electronics engineer and inventor, Christopher Cockerell will be best remembered for his invention of the hovercraft, which has carried millions of passengers across the English Channel since its launch in 1968. A key member of the Marconi working on the development of radar during World War Two, he went on to patent nearly 100 inventions in a career spanning 64 years.

Educated at Cambridge University, Cockerell joined the Marconi Wireless Telegraph Company as an electronics engineer in 1935 and was involved in developing airborne and navigational equipment. He devised 36 inventions, notably a two-needle aerial direction finder, nicknamed 'the drunken men', a device which brought thousands of airmen safely home during the war.

In 1951 he left Marconi to purchase a small boat-building business on the Norfolk Broads. A keen amateur yachtsman, he began working on ways to reduce friction between a boat's hull and the water, to make it go faster. He decided to try the radical solution of raising the boat's hull completely out of the water, and embarked on two years of painstaking research. The breakthrough came in 1953 when, by performing an experiment with a set of kitchen scales, an industrial air-blower and two empty food tins, he confirmed his calculations that the air cushion created would provide the necessary lift, and thus the basis for a revolutionary new vessel, the amphibious 'hovercraft', was born.

Cockerell was granted a patent in 1955, and three years later the National Research and Development Corporation commissioned the Isle of Wight company Saunders-Roe Ltd to build a full-size prototype. The two-seater SR-N1 was launched in 1959 and, with its inventor stationed outboard as ballast, made its first Channel crossing from Calais to Dover. Cockerell was appointed technical director of Hovercraft Development Ltd, and oversaw the research and development work which led to the introduction of viable commercial hovercraft. Awarded the CBE in 1966, he was also elected a Fellow of the Royal Society and awarded their Royal Gold Medal.

Knighted in 1969, Cockerell patented numerous inventions over the years and was working on new ideas until a few months before his death in June 1999.

Many people have ideas, but I would say that in order to convert ideas into realities, it is necessary to have a lot of luck, time, facilities and the ability to live on air. One must not be born too late or too early, or in the wrong place; and if the idea has anything to do with marine experts, it is wise to plan to live for a very long time.

BETTY BOOTHROYD

The Rt. Hon. Betty Boothroyd MP
Born 1929, Dewsbury, Yorkshire

Betty Boothroyd occupies a unique position in British political history as the first female Speaker of the House of Commons. Known as 'Madam Speaker', and famously refusing to wear the traditional wig, she has controlled parliamentary proceedings with a blend of firmness, impartiality and good humour.

The daughter of Yorkshire mill-workers who were active members of the Labour Party, Boothroyd was educated at Dewsbury College of Commerce and Art. A politically active party member in her teens, she moved to London in 1947, aged 18, to pursue her childhood passion for dance, and performed with the Tiller Girls for three months before heading home to become a secretary. She returned to London to work for Party HQ at Transport House and then became parliamentary secretary to MPs Barbara Castle and Geoffrey de Freitas. Following an unsuccessful attempt to stand as a candidate in 1957 she left for America to work on John F. Kennedy's presidential campaign, and stayed on after his election, working as a legislative assistant in the House of Representatives.

Back in Britain in 1961, Boothroyd fought four parliamentary elections before becoming MP for West Bromwich in the 1973 by-election. A year later she won West Bromwich West for Labour, a seat she has held ever since. Also in 1974, she became assistant whip for the Labour Party and went on to become a member of the European Parliament. She served on the House of Commons Select Committee on Foreign Affairs, and in 1981 was appointed to the party's National Executive Committee, where she rapidly established herself as the 'Hammer of the Left'. Six years later she became one of three Deputy Speakers of the Commons, and in 1992 she was elected Speaker, the first to be chosen from the opposition benches since 1835.

Awarded the Freedom of the City of London in 1993, Boothroyd has received numerous honorary degrees and is patron of a wide range of organisations, including the Westminster Foundation for Democracy. She was re-elected Speaker in 1997.

Is there so great a superfluity of men fit for high duties, that society can afford to reject the service of any competent person? Are we so certain of always finding a man made to our hands for any duty or function of social importance which falls vacant, that we lose nothing by putting a ban upon one-half of mankind, and refusing beforehand to make their faculties available, however distinguished they may be?
John Stuart Mill, *The Subjection of Women*, 1859

ROBIN DAY

Sir Robin Day
Born 1923, London

The acclaimed 'First Knight of the Box', political journalist Robin Day has been the foremost interviewer of the television era. With his trademark spectacles, bow-tie, and dogged determination to ask the questions the masses want answering, he is credited with developing a vigorous and incisive style which has served to make him a formidable inquisitor of seven Prime Ministers from MacMillan to Major.

The son of a post office engineer, Day served in the Royal Artillery during World War Two and studied law at St Edmund Hall, Oxford. He was called to the Bar in 1952 but, after two years, decided to pursue a career in broadcasting, joining the fledgling Independent Television News (ITN) as a newscaster in 1955. He established his credentials with his coverage of the Suez Crisis in 1956, his first big political assignment, and won the Guild of Television Producers and Directors Award for his landmark interview with Egypt's President Nasser in 1957.

In 1959 he joined the BBC's flagship current affairs programme, *Panorama*, as a political correspondent covering international news, and remained a key contributor for 30 years. He took the helm at BBC Radio 4's lunchtime news programme, *The World at One*, from 1979 to 1987, and reached the zenith of his broadcasting career when he became chairman of the BBC's political debate programme, *Question Time* in 1979. His role, originally intended as a six-month 'filler', grew into a ten-year tenure, during which time his acerbic wit and fierce intellect famously trounced disingenuous or evasive politicians on his panel.

Knighted in 1981, Day has been at the forefront of the BBC's television coverage of nine general elections in his 40-year career, and has received numerous awards for broadcasting, including the Richard Dimbleby Award in 1975 and the RTS 'Judges' Award in 1985. He published his best-selling memoirs, *Grand Inquisitor*, in 1989, and produced a collection of interviews with parliamentarians and others, *...But With Respect*, in 1993. *Speaking for Myself*, a collection of speeches, was published in 1999.

'The world continues to offer glittering prizes to those who have stout hearts and sharp swords.'
F.E Smith, Earl of Birkenhead, 1923.

BRUCE KENT

Bruce Kent
Born 1929, London

Activist, dissident and Catholic priest, Bruce Kent is a peace campaigner and the recognised flagbearer of the Campaign for Nuclear Disarmament (CND).

Kent studied at Oxford University and spent six years in a seminary before being ordained in the diocese of Westminster in 1958. He served as a curate in London until 1963, before becoming secretary in the Archbishop's House, Westminster, and then Catholic chaplain to London University in 1966. As a young curate, he joined the Catholic peace organisation Pax Christi, and as a result of his increasing concern about the morality of nuclear weapons, became a member of CND. In 1977 he became a parish priest in Euston, London.

When the government announced in 1979 that it would welcome the stationing of American cruise missiles in Britain, and that it intended to replace its Polaris nuclear system with Trident submarines, Kent resigned from his parish to become General Secretary of CND. He took his pulpit to Trafalgar Square and in so doing became a key figure in the dramatic revival of the peace movement in the 1980s, with rallies attracting hundreds of thousands of people. One of the co-ordinators of the British UN Disarmament Week demonstration in Hyde Park in October 1981, to which more than 250,000 people flocked, Kent became one of the best-known Catholic priests in Britain and the face of the CND movement.

In 1987, aware of the growing conflict between his political and religious beliefs, Kent retired from the priesthood and began to campaign internationally to increase awareness of the threat of nuclear weapons and to urge nations to accept the fight for peace as a global responsibility. In 1985 he succeeded Sean MacBride as President of the International Peace Bureau, a post he held until 1992. Vice-President of CND and Pax Christi, Kent is also active in the Forum for UN Renewal and Abolition 2000 UK, the aim of which is to abolish nuclear weapons worldwide.

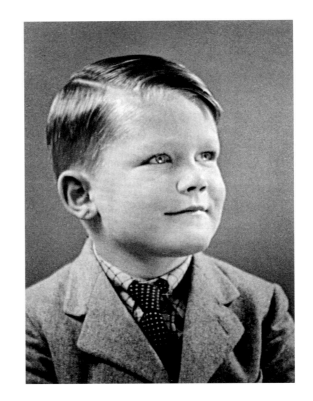

One day it is going to dawn on the human race that war is as barbaric a means of resolving conflict as cannibalism is as a means of coping with diet deficiency. If we had only read the right parts of the right books we might have learned that long ago:
'A King is not saved by his great army.
A warrior is not delivered by his great strength.
The war horse is a vain hope for victory
and by its great strength it cannot save.' Psalm 33

BARBARA CARTLAND

Dame Barbara Cartland
Born 1901, Worcestershire

The doyenne of romantic fiction, Barbara Cartland is the world's best-selling author, with over 700 titles to her name and book sales in excess of 650 million. A devotee of traditional values such as chivalry, honour and chastity before marriage, she has dictated, on average, a love-story per fortnight for the past 28 years, and been a staunch campaigner for humanitarian and charitable causes for over 70 years.

The daughter of aristocrat James Cartland, who was killed in the First World War, Cartland wrote, illustrated and bound her first book, *The Little Slide Maker*, aged just five. Educated at boarding school in Malvern, by private governess in Somerset and at a finishing school in Southampton, she famously received the first of 49 marriage proposals nine days after leaving school.

A debutante in 1920s London, she published her first novel, *Jigsaw*, in 1923 to instant acclaim. Described as 'Mayfair with the lid off', it ran into six editions and was translated into five languages. Inaugurating her writing career with the mission to bring a touch of glamour and romance to the world, she set a prolific pace, producing novels such as *Not Love Alone* (1933) and *Passionate Attainment* (1935), as well as contributing articles to newspapers and magazines. A high society hostess and active charity fund-raiser throughout the war years, Cartland joined the Women's Voluntary Service in 1940 and the St. John's Ambulance Brigade in 1943, becoming Commander of the Order of St. John of Jerusalem in 1953, by which time she had published her 50th novel. In 1958 she campaigned for improved salaries and conditions for midwives and nurses, and in 1962 precipitated a change in housing law to benefit the welfare of Britain's gypsy communities. She founded the National Association for Health in 1964, promoting vitamins and herbal medicines, recorded an album of love songs with the Royal Philharmonic Orchestra and published her 200th book, *No Escape From Love*, in 1978.

A multi-award winning novelist and playwright, Cartland has had numerous adaptations of her work televised. She has published widely her philosophies on love, health, beauty and guides to relationships, and penned historical books on the private lives of several monarchs. She was awarded the DBE in 1991.

One thing I know, life can never die.
Translucent, splendid, flaming like the sun.
Only our bodies wither and deny
The life force when our strength is done.

Let me transmit this wonderful fire,
Even a little through my heart and mind,
Bringing the perfect love we all desire
To those who seek, yet blindly cannot find.

From *Lines on Life and Love*, by Cartland, 1972

QUINTIN HOGG

The Rt. Hon. Lord Hailsham of St. Marylebone CH. FRS
Born 1907, London

Quintin Hogg is the longest-serving Lord Chancellor and longest-serving cabinet minister this century, having occupied senior posts in the governments of five Conservative prime ministers from Winston Churchill to Sir Alec Douglas-Home.

The son of the 1st Viscount Hailsham, himself a Lord Chancellor, Hogg studied at Oxford University and was called to the Bar in 1932. An admirer of Neville Chamberlain, he was elected to the House of Commons after standing as a 'pro-Munich' candidate in the 1938 Oxford by-election, but finally voted against the government in the Norway debate of 1940, which brought Churchill to power. He remained the member for Oxford City until 1950 when, on the death of his father, he inherited the title of the 2nd Viscount Hailsham, and took his seat in the House of Lords. He was appointed First Lord of the Admiralty in 1956 and became Minister of Education in 1957. He was Chairman of the Conservative Party (1957-59) and Lord President of the Council (1957-59), before serving as Minister for Science and Technology (1959-64).

Hogg led the British negotiating team in the nuclear test ban treaty of Moscow in 1963, and was Harold Macmillan's chosen successor in the party leadership contest that year. He renounced his peerage to stand for the leadership but was defeated by Douglas-Home. Re-elected to the Commons in the St. Marylebone by-election, he served as Secretary of State for Education and Science in 1964 and became Shadow Home Secretary two years later. In 1970 he was appointed both a Life Peer and Lord Chancellor, serving his first term until 1974, during which time he established himself as a staunch defender of the Bar against threats to its rights and privileges. He oversaw the launch of the Green Form Scheme, which extended the provision of legal aid, and during his second term as Lord Chancellor (1979-87), introduced legally aided advice and assistance for suspects detained at police stations. He also voiced his growing concern about the power of a strong government, castigating it as an 'elective dictatorship'.

Esteemed for his intellect, Hailsham has written widely on aspects of the British legal and political systems throughout his career.

The best way I know to win an argument is to start by being in the right.

Main photograph: 30th July 1998, Putney, London
Inset photograph: Aged 21, in the Lake District

JULIE ANDREWS

Julie Andrews
Born Julia Elizabeth Wells, 1935, Walton-on-Thames, Surrey

Julie Andrews was a child star who became one of Britain's first international musical and film stars, best known for her legendary performances in the classic 1960s films *Mary Poppins* and *The Sound of Music*. Renowned for her crystal clear voice, wholesome looks and innate poise, she has combined award-winning film and stage roles with television shows, concerts and recordings over the past 50 years.

Andrews began singing lessons aged eight, honing an already remarkable vocal range, and eventually joined her parents in their Vaudeville act, touring the music halls billed as 'England's Juvenile Singing Sensation'. She made her professional stage debut in the *Starlight Roof* revue at the London Hippodrome in 1947, aged 12, and became a regular performer on BBC radio and in pantomime. Her fresh-faced innocence as Cinderella in 1953, aged 18, caught the eye of a director casting for the Broadway production of the successful London musical, *The Boy Friend*, and she left for America to play the lead ingenue, Polly Browne, in 1954. It was a smash hit, and she followed it by creating the role of Eliza Doolittle in the award-winning Lerner-Lowe musical *My Fair Lady* in 1956.

A lead role as Queen Guinevere opposite Richard Burton's King Arthur in *Camelot* on Broadway from 1960-62 was followed by an invitation from Walt Disney to star in his ambitious new, live-action movie musical, *Mary Poppins*. Her magical portrayal of the prim, whimsical, all-singing, all-dancing British nanny was a spectacular success and she won the Oscar for Best Actress in 1964. A year later she played Maria Von Trapp in the Rodgers and Hammerstein musical film *The Sound of Music* (1965), which broke all box office records and remains one of the most enduringly popular family entertainment films.

Starring roles in films such as *Hawaii* (1966) and *Thoroughly Modern Millie* (1967) were followed by *Star!* (1968) and *Darling Lili* (1970), amongst others, and in 1972 her television series, *The Julie Andrews Hour*, won seven Emmys, including one for Best Variety Show. Further film roles include *10* (1979), the musical farce *Victor/Victoria* (1982), in which Andrews excelled as a transvestite, and *That's Life* (1985), all directed by her second husband Blake Edwards. In 1986 she played a concert violinist stricken with multiple sclerosis in the film *Duet for One* (1986) and in 1995 she returned to Broadway for a sell-out, 18-month run of the stage version of *Victor/Victoria*.

People tell me I'm very disciplined. For me, discipline provides a foundation that leaves me free to fly.

Main photograph: 6th June 1999, New York, USA
Inset photograph: Aged 9

LINFORD CHRISTIE

Linford Christie OBE
Born 1960, St Andrews, Jamaica

Champion Olympic sprinter Linford Christie is a sportsman venerated for his mesmerising athletic ability. In an international career spanning 18 years he has competed over 60 times for Britain, won 23 major championship medals, which is more than any other British male athlete, set European and British records in the 100 metres event and is the only European sprinter to have broken the 10-second barrier in the 100 metres.

Christie came to London at the age of seven and began competing in school athletics, making his international debut for Great Britain against Germany in 1980, aged 19. In 1982 he began training with the Thames Valley Harriers and in 1986 he won his first gold medal as the unexpected victor in the 200 metres race at the European Indoor Championships in Madrid. Six months later, at the European Outdoor Championships in Stuttgart, he won the first of three successive European 100m titles.

In 1988 he won silver at the Seoul Olympics in both the 100 metres and 4 x 100 metres relay events, as well as setting a British and European 100 metres record of 9.92 seconds and a British 200 metre record of 20.09 seconds. In 1990 he claimed his second 100 metres title in the European Championships and his first Commonwealth Games 100 metres gold medal.

Christie reached the pinnacle of his career at the 1992 Barcelona Olympics when he captained the British men's team and won the 100 metres gold medal, aged 32, displacing Allan Wells as the oldest man to take the title. A year later he won the 100 metres gold medal at the World Championships in Stuttgart, achieving his fastest ever time of 9.87 seconds, which remains the European record. In 1996 he was disqualified from the finals of the 100 metres event at the Atlanta Olympics for two false-starts, but won gold in the 1997 Europa Cup 100 and 200 metres before retiring from international athletics.

Awarded the OBE in 1998, Christie remains an inspirational figure in the world of sport and coaches some of Britain's leading international athletes. He commentates on athletics for television and hosts the BBC programme *Linford's Record Breakers*.

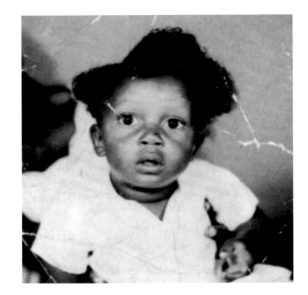

'How can you discover the ocean if you are afraid to leave the shore?'

Main photograph: 29th October 1998, London
Inset photograph: Aged 2

RICHARD ROGERS

Lord Rogers of Riverside RA, MArch., RIBA
Born 1933, Florence, Italy

Charged with the design of Britain's gargantuan monument to the new millennium, the £750 million Dome on the tip of the Greenwich Peninsula, Richard Rogers is one of the most flamboyant and controversial architects of our time. Creator of dynamic, hi-tech buildings, he is a passionate promoter of civic responsibility and the development of vibrant public spaces where communities can thrive.

Rogers came to Britain in 1938 and studied at the Architectural Association in London and Yale University before establishing Team 4 with Norman Foster, Su Rogers and Wendy Cheesman in 1963. Following their success with the design of the Reliance Controls building in Swindon in 1967, Rogers teamed up with the Italian architect Renzo Piano and shot to international fame in 1971 with his design for the Centre National d'Art et de Culture Georges Pompidou in Paris, a glass-walled 'climbing-frame' with a striking exterior of structural and service elements encased in brightly coloured tubes, completed in 1977. Hailed as the most successful modern building in the world by some, and derided as an eyesore by others, it has become a tourist attraction in France second only to the Eiffel Tower.

The Richard Rogers Partnership was established in 1983, and its modern, functionalist and gregarious designs for high-profile, public buildings have aroused both admiration and controversy. The Lloyd's Building, a gleaming, dramatic construct of steel and glass that opened in 1986, also with its air-conditioning and plumbing stacked on the exterior, and the Channel 4 television HQ at Victoria, both in London, are celebrated as fine examples of modern British architecture. Prestigious commissions throughout the 90s have included the European Court of Human Rights in Strasbourg, completed in 1995, the law courts in Bordeaux, completed in 1998, and the fifth terminal for London's Heathrow airport.

An ardent socialist, committed to sustainable urban planning that maximises the social potential, Rogers is Chairman of the Architecture Foundation and the Urban Task Force. He was knighted in 1991 and created a Labour Peer in 1996.

People make cities but cities make citizens. The condition of our cities cannot be ignored because the lesson of history is that, depending upon the quality of life they offer, they can and will humanise or brutalise their inhabitants.

Main photograph: 13th August 1998, Chelsea, London
Inset photograph: Aged 7, Italy

MARY WHITEHOUSE

Mary Whitehouse CBE
Born 1910, Chester

Mary Whitehouse has led a spirited campaign for the maintenance of Christian values and moral decency in British society for the past 30 years. Founder and President Emeritus of the National Viewers and Listeners Association (NVLA) in 1964, she set out to monitor the effects of broadcasting and the mass media on society and to legislate for the control of obscenity and pornography in the media.

Educated in Cheshire, it was as Senior Mistress at the Madeley Secondary Modern School in Shropshire from 1960-64 that she was first required to be responsible for the moral welfare of her charges, and to become involved in what was then the new venture of sex education. The 1962 Newsom Report on Secondary Education believed that sex education should be based on 'chastity before marriage and fidelity within it', a view held by Whitehouse herself, and its instruction to the teenagers in her care was the start of a lifelong commitment to spread the word. Her conviction that violence on television inevitably results in a violent society was the basis of her 1964 'Clean Up TV Campaign' and remained a key principle in her subsequent work.

Sustained lobbying by NVLA members throughout the 70s and 80s led to the passing of significant legislation, including the 1979 Protection of Children Act, supported by 1.6 million signatures on a petition against child pornography, and the 1981 Indecent Displays Act. A regular commentator on news programmes and a lecturer on the university circuit, Whitehouse famously took out a private prosecution against the National Theatre's controversial production of *Romans in Britain* in 1981, before co-ordinating the campaign to establish the Broadcasting Standards Council in 1989, one of the NVLA's most important victories.

She retired as president in 1994, having built a substantial membership within the organisation to continue the fight for better broadcasting standards.

A nation's youth is its greatest asset. We are poor guardians if we do not ensure its inalienable right to childhood, mystery, dreams, tenderness and love; if we do not realize that by ceasing to provide authority we may also cease to care; if we do not conscientiously maintain the spiritual foundations without which the young cannot build anew; if we do not teach that there is a third way, neither reactionary nor libertarian, which still waits to be explored.

GEORGE MARTIN

Sir George Martin CBE
Born 1926, London

Legendary music producer George Martin is best known as the man who signed The Beatles when every other record label in England had turned them down. One of the most versatile and influential figures in the music business over the last 50 years, his ability to nurture talent and champion new musical styles has resulted in a record 30 Number One hit singles.

After graduating from the Guildhall School of Music in 1949, Martin worked as a professional oboe player in London before beginning his career as a producer with EMI in 1950. He was appointed Head of the Parlophone label in 1955 and worked with jazz artists such as John Dankworth and Humphrey Lyttleton, as well as producing hit comedy albums, such as *The Goon Shows* (1959) and *Beyond the Fringe* (1961).

In 1962, on a hunch, he signed an unknown band from Liverpool called The Beatles, producing their debut single, *Love Me Do*, which became a top 20 UK hit, followed by their first Number One album, *Please Please Me*, in 1963. Harnessing the natural songwriting talents of Lennon and McCartney, Martin presided over a string of ground-breaking Beatles records, including the epochal *Sergeant Pepper's Lonely Hearts Club Band* (1967), Britain's biggest selling album to date, which have come to be regarded as the biggest single influence on popular culture since the advent of rock'n'roll itself.

In 1969 he set up AIR Studios, which rapidly became one of the world's most successful recording centres, and produced a diverse range of music as well as composing 15 film scores, including *A Hard Day's Night* (1964) and the Bond film *Live and Let Die* (1973), for which he won a Grammy Award. Honoured with the CBE in 1988, Martin won his fifth Grammy Award for the album of Pete Townshend's hit show *Tommy* in 1994, and in 1995 produced *The Beatles Anthology* collections, containing studio out-takes and rare recordings, which have sold over 10 million copies.

Knighted in 1996, he produced *Candle in the Wind* in 1997, Elton John's tribute to Diana, the late Princess of Wales, and a year later, completed *In My Life*, his final album before retiring. A compilation of specially recorded tracks performed by The Beatles and a variety of other singers and actors, it has since 'gone gold' in Britain, Australia and Canada.

Music is the most sublime of all the arts. It's the most intangible, it's a mystery, and it's been with us since we were primeval. Human beings were making music eighty thousand years ago, before they could talk. I think it's the most fundamental part of our lives; in fact, without rhythm, we wouldn't exist. Your heart is pumping out a rhythm, and when it stops you don't live any more, so rhythm is actually the difference between life and death...

Main photograph: 23rd July 1998, London
Inset photograph: Aged 10

MARGARET THATCHER

The Rt. Hon. Baroness Thatcher of Kesteven in the County of Lincolnshire LG. OM. FRS
Born Margaret Roberts. 1925. Grantham. Lincolnshire

Margaret Thatcher holds the unique position of being the first woman Prime Minister of Britain and the leader of the longest uninterrupted government this century. The architect of a radical conservatism which promoted the free market, private enterprise and the diminution of trade unionism, she transformed the economy and ushered in a new era in British politics.

The daughter of a grocer, Thatcher was educated at Oxford University and became a research chemist in 1947, before studying law and being called to the Bar in 1954. She was elected Conservative MP for Finchley in 1959 and was appointed joint Parliamentary Secretary to the then Ministry of Pensions and National Insurance in 1961. Following the Conservative victory of 1970 she was made Secretary of State for Education and Science and soon established a reputation as a fiscal hard-liner. When Labour came to power in 1974 she was appointed Shadow Chancellor, and in 1975 she defeated Edward Heath to become party leader.

Thatcher became Prime Minister in 1979 with a Conservative manifesto based on curbing the power of the unions and cutting inflation. She swiftly passed laws which effectively paralysed the unions and drastically cut public spending, with the result that the economy prospered for a period, until rising unemployment, particularly in the manufacturing industries, and cuts in welfare benefits sparked accusations that she lacked compassion. However her uncompromising stance during the Falklands War, when Britain recaptured the islands from Argentina in 1982, boosted her popularity and she was re-elected in 1983, after which she initiated her programme of privatisation of state utilities.

Dubbed the 'Iron Lady' for her fiercely anti-Communist stance on foreign affairs, Thatcher created close links with America, but remained distant from Europe. Re-elected for a third term in 1987, her introduction of the Community Charge in 1989 met with mass public hostility, and her opposition to European integration, which ran counter to the views of most of her cabinet, contributed to an increasing alienation from her colleagues. The resignation of her Chancellor, Nigel Lawson, in 1989 and Foreign Secretary, Geoffrey Howe, in 1990, sparked a leadership challenge by Michael Heseltine, and she was forced to stand down in November of that year.

Retiring from Parliament in 1992, she established the Thatcher Foundation to promote free enterprise and democracy worldwide. Awarded the Order of Merit in 1990 and created a Life Peer in 1992, Baroness Thatcher will be remembered as a formidable leader whose 11 years in power have left an indelible mark on British political history.

Eternal spirit of the chainless mind!
Brightest in dungeons. Liberty! Thou art.
For there thy habitation is the heart -
The heart which love of thee alone can bind...
From *Sonnet on Chillon* by Lord Byron (1788-1824)

JOHN CLEESE

John Cleese
Born 1939, Weston-super-Mare

'Minister of Silly Walks', John Cleese is one of Britain's most successful and best-loved comic talents. A writer and performer, he is most famous for his creation of Basil Fawlty, the hotel manager from hell, in the BBC's vintage television series Fawlty Towers, and is a key member of the team who produced Monty Python's Flying Circus.

Humour is emotional chaos recalled in tranquility.
James Thurber

Main photograph: 4th November 1998, Pinewood Studios, Buckinghamshire
Inset photograph: In the school cricket team

LESTER PIGGOTT

Lester Piggott
Born 1935, Wantage, Berkshire

Lester Piggott is widely regarded as the world's greatest jockey, having achieved unparalleled success in horse racing history during a six-decade career. The youngest ever winner of the Derby, aged just 18, he went on to become champion jockey 11 times, winning a record nine Derbys and 30 Classic races.

The son of champion jockey Keith Piggott, he was born and bred to ride, and made his professional debut in 1948, aged just 12, riding his first winner later that year. In 1950, aged 14, he was ranked 11th in the list of most successful British jockeys, and in 1954 he won his first Derby, riding *Never Say Die*. He established a successful partnership with legendary trainer Noel Murless from 1955 to 1966, becoming Champion jockey for the first time in 1960, and rapidly generated a reputation for single-mindedness and a ruthless determination to win.

Dubbed 'The Long Fellow' because at 5' 7" he was unusually tall for a jockey, Piggott famously maintained a diet of tea and cigars to keep his weight down. He was rewarded with continued Derby successes on horses such as *St Paddy* (1960), *Nijinsky* (1970), *The Minstrel* (1977) and *Teenoso* (1983) and was nick-named the 'Housewives' Choice' after achieving well over 4,000 victories in Britain between 1955 and 1985. Having become officially freelance in 1967, he triumphed abroad, winning the French Prix de l'Arc de Triomphe on *Rheingold* in 1973, and on Alleged in 1977 and 1978, and seized victory at the Washington DC International on *Sir Ivor* (1968), *Karabas* (1969) and *Argument* (1980).

In 1985 he retired to become a racehorse trainer, but made a comeback in 1990, sensationally winning the Breeders' Cup Mile in the USA before retiring for good in 1995. Having maintained peak fitness and performance until the remarkable age of 60, Piggott has enjoyed a momentous career in which he has won the St Leger eight times, the Oaks six times, the 2000 Guineas five times and the 1000 Guineas twice.

Never say die!

INDEX

ACKNOWLEDGEMENTS

It was clear from the start that there would be a vacancy for angels.

Fortunately, they alighted in droves. I would like to express my gratitude to the following people who put their faith in me from the beginning:

John Pitchforth, gentle man, who took a risk, handed over the Rolleiflex and started the ball rolling; Neil Hargreaves at KJP, who gave me lighting, film, technical support and non-stop encouragement; Gavin Finney and Karole Lange, who lent me back-up equipment and then 'forgot' to need it back; Andrew Leci, who helped me seize the moment; and Stuart Smith, who gave his time and skill to a stranger, because he knows about dreams.

Thank you to Jonathan Freedland, Anthony Julius, Laurie Milner, Ian Hodge, Robert McCrum, Julian Forrester, Peter Connors, Nick Sinclair, Robert Khodadad, Jane Merkin, Robert Kirby, Peter Cork, Barrie Gill, Arthur Farndell, Alison Gatoff and Asa Briggs, who generously gave of their time and expertise throughout.

I am grateful to David Morgan for his kindness and patience during the difficult early days, and to Greg Rack, for casting *Centurions* afloat.

My assistants Cara Viereckl, Troy Lilley, Mike Fieldhouse and Bridget Peirson were models of patience and loyalty, and I thank them for their hard work. My printers Debbie Sears at Metro Art and Peter Guest at The Image were extremely generous with their time and skill, under pressure, and I am grateful for their kindness. My thanks, also, to the staff of KJP's Rental Department, Joe's Basement Ltd. and Stopwatch Publishing Ltd. for all their cooperation.

I am delighted that Nicola Horlick, John Richards, Rufus Warner and John Ions of SG Asset Management leapt aboard this project with such enthusiasm, and I thank them for their appreciation of my work.

Very special thanks to my sisters Sharon Pink and Laura Djanogly, for their ceaseless encouragement and support, and to my mum, Lee, for always holding it, and us, together.

My close friends and colleagues gave me their unwavering support and encouragement throughout the making of this book, for which I am deeply touched and grateful.

I would like to thank my subjects for giving me their time, and allowing me to raid their photograph albums, and I would particularly like to thank, and apologise to, those I have been unable to include, due to the limited number of pages.

Centurions would not have been started without the kindness of my father, Maurice Djanogly. It would not have been finished without the phenomenal hard work and loyalty of Natalie Walsh. Thank you, both of you, for your love and friendship.

Finally, I would like to extend my heartfelt gratitude to the two men without whose kindness this book would not have come into the world. Elliot and Jonathan Lewis, your generosity, commitment and faith have touched me beyond words. From the bottom of my heart, I thank you for believing in me.

ILLUSTRATIONS

Stanley Matthews, p.40, courtesy of Staffordshire
    Sentinel Newspapers

Tom Kliburn, p.92, reprinted with permission of the
    Department of Computer Science, University of
    Manchester

Tanni Grey, p.136, by Gray Mortimore, Allsport.

Tom Stoppard, p.164, by Colin Davey, Camera Press Ltd

Iris Murdoch, p.170, by Steve Brodie, Times
    Newspapers Ltd.

Arthur C. Clarke, p.182, courtesy of Rocket
    Publishing/Science and Society Picture Library

Lester Piggott, p.210, by Douglas Hooper

EXTRACTS

P.16, Extract from *The Man with the Blue Guitar* by
    Wallace Stevens, 1936

P.28, Extract from *Worstward Ho* by Samuel Beckett,
    reproduced by permission of The Samuel Beckett
    Estate 1983, 1999

P.34, Extract from *A Naive and Sentimental Lover* by
    John Le Carre, reproduced by permission of Hodder
    and Stoughton Ltd.

P.70, *Polliciti Melliora* by Frank Thompson, reproduced
    with permission granted by E.P Thompson to The
    Salamander Trust

P.78, *Johnny Head-in-Air* by John Pudney,
    Selected Poems, published by J.M.Dent, reprinted
    by permission of David Higham Associates.

P.116, Extract from *The Engima of Arrival* © 1987
    V.S.Naipaul. Reprinted with the permission of Gillon
    Aitken Associates Ltd.

P.122, Extract from *If*, by Rudyard Kipling, reprinted
    by permission of A.P Watt Ltd on behalf of The
    National Trust for Places of Historic Interest or
    Natural Beauty.

P.178, Extract from *Secret Theatre* by Robert Graves,
    reprinted by permission of Carcanet Press Ltd.